CW00326385

Success in Spelling

by
Patrick McLaughlin

SCHOFIELD & SIMS LTD. HUDDERSFIELD ENGLAND

First printed 1994

0 7217 0675 4
Net edition 0 7217 0691 6

Designed and typeset by Armitage Typo/Graphics Ltd., Huddersfield
Printed in Great Britain by Scotprint, Musselburgh

Contents

Contents

4

Contents

Introduction

HOW WE CAN IMPROVE OUR SPELLING

It is the function of **Success in Spelling** to allow people to improve their spelling either by their own efforts or through the mediation of a good teacher.

This book will:

- Produce a detailed and simple system for self-diagnosis and the solving of individual spelling problems.

- Demonstrate that English spelling is not as irregular and difficult as is often imagined.

- Point out that the total number of words involved in each element of the spelling system is not large in most cases and can be learnt.

- Emphasise that the physical act of writing the words is part of the spelling process.

SPELLING RULES

It is popularly supposed that English spelling is something of a mess with few rules that make any real sense and a bewildering number of exceptions. *The reverse of this is nearer the truth*. One of the reasons why this is not properly appreciated is because of the very poor formulation of the rules by many people. Much confusion springs from this. It is pleasing to most learners to discover that English spelling is more systematic than they thought.

LISTS OF WORDS

In this book lists of words are included with all the rules. These lists are, for the most part, comprehensive. They are based on the most frequently occurring words and encompass a vocabulary list that is adequate for most people's needs. The lists do not include specialised or very uncommon words but otherwise are comprehensive. If you knew how to spell all such words you would be highly efficient over the whole range of normal vocabulary.

8

These lists are not as extensive and intimidating as you may have thought. The number of root words containing **ie** / **ei**, for example, amounts to only fifty words and five or six exceptions. *You could easily learn all of these words in a single session.* The same applies to almost all the other elements of the spelling system. Listing together all the words that come into a particular class (such as the **-ible** words) allows for easy reference and brings together words that you would only otherwise encounter in reading a large number of texts over a lengthy period of time.

EXERCISES

In the exercises that accompany each unit the pupil is encouraged to write out the lists of words shown. The purpose of this is to give vital practice in writing the words, to get the 'feel' of the words in the hand. Further practice is provided by giving the pupil the opportunity to use selected words from the lists in sentences of their own.

HOW TO USE THIS BOOK

It would be possible to use this book as the basis of a complete course of spelling, going through the units one by one in whatever order. However, this is not the use we envisage for this book. At the stage we are dealing with it is seldom necessary for someone to learn anew all the different elements of the spelling system; few people are quite that bad. Usually people have particular problems in their spelling, of which there may be many, but there are aspects of spelling that do not give trouble. The intention is to identify the pupil's particular spelling problems and then to use the appropriate sections of the book.

TEACHING METHODS

Any scheme for the improvement of spelling must be based upon the needs of individuals. The teaching of spelling tends to be geared to whole class instruction, yet class teaching in this area can be wasteful of time and resources. To teach a whole class some element of spelling is usually to guarantee that most of your effort will be wasted. There will be many in the class who have no problem with that particular item. There will be others for whom this is not the most pressing problem. Though the teacher is standing in front of 30 pupils he may be really only contacting two or three. To avoid this, spelling should be taught to individuals, based on their own identified and assessed needs.

First of all, there should be a diagnostic system. This system should be simple and effective. It must be capable of being carried out by the pupils themselves. It should lead the pupils to identify their own needs and priorities and then take control of their own follow-up work. Effectively, this frees the teacher for the supervisory role of giving advice and help to individuals working on their own self-identified programmes. Furthermore, the teacher will have a record supplied to him or her by the pupil. This will pinpoint areas of weakness rather than simply giving a 'score'.

SELF-DIAGNOSTIC SYSTEM

STEP 1

Pupils collect all their *corrected* written work over a significant period. It can include their writing in any subject in the curriculum so long as this has been corrected and the spelling mistakes marked.

STEP 2

The pupils are each given a large sheet of paper (Sheet 1) and have beside them their pile of exercise books. Quite simply, the pupil extracts from each exercise book in turn, page by page, each word he or she has misspelt and copies these words onto the sheet. At this stage it doesn't matter whether it is a corrected or uncorrected version of the word. It is important that every word is recorded and *on each and every occasion it is met*, no matter how often the same word is being copied onto the sheet. At the end of this session, say an hour at most, the pupil will have a single sheet that contains all the spelling mistakes over a significant period of time and many pieces of work. Whatever problems the pupil has, whatever the pattern of his or her errors, it is all there in unsorted form.

STEP 3

The pupils are given another large sheet of paper. Each pupil transfers the words on Sheet 1 to Sheet 2. This time, however, he or she writes each word, *one after the other along the top* of Sheet 2. Whenever a word is met which is the same as a word at the top of Sheet 2 then this is placed underneath that word. As each word is entered on Sheet 2, it is crossed out on Sheet 1. The final result is a sheet that has something like the following pattern:

SHEET 2

word 1	word 2	word 3	word 4	word 5	word 6	word 7	word 8
word 1	word 2	word 3	word 4	word 5	word 6	word 7	word 8
word 1	word 2	word 3	word 4		word 6		word 8
word 1	word 2		word 4		word 6		
word 1			word 4		word 6		
word 1			word 4				
word 1			word 4				
word 1							
word 1							
word 1							

Both pupil and teacher can tell *at a glance* which words are causing problems. The priorities for follow-up establish themselves. The longest columns indicate the most pervasive errors but also give the promise of the most dramatic improvements in overall performance.

THE FOLLOW-UP

When a particular problem is identified by means of this diagnostic system, then the pupil goes to the place in this book where that aspect of spelling is dealt with and works on it until it is understood and ceases to be a problem. The pupil should expect not to make the same mistakes again. Complete mastery of each element is the aim.

THE BENEFITS OF THIS SYSTEM

These are:

- The pupil develops and controls his or her own diagnostic/remedial programme.
- The pupil learns valuable research and time-management skills.
- The teacher coordinates the research and follow-up programme and has the time to give personal attention to those pupils who need it.
- The teacher, the school and the parents have the opportunity to be well-informed about the individual problems and the steps being taken to resolve them. This should assist greatly in home/school integration.

PART 1

Forming Plurals

1 RULE
To form the plural of a word you normally add -s to the singular.

EXAMPLE

Singular			*Plural*
pencil	+ s	=	pencils

EXERCISE

■ Add -s to the following words using the above rule.

bell	coin	elephant	giraffe	girl	leak
level	mile	orange	palace	primrose	spark
team	umbrella	wreck	year		

2 RULE
You add -es to the singular to form the plural of words ending in -o, -s, -x, -ch or -sh.

a RULE
Words ending in -o add -es to form the plural.

EXAMPLE

Singular			*Plural*
halo	+ es	=	haloes
▲	▲		
ends in -o	add -es		

12

■ Copy out the list below in your workbook *three* times.

halo	haloes
motto	mottoes
potato	potatoes
tomato	tomatoes

■ Learn this list off by heart.

■ With a partner, test each other's knowledge of the list.

EXCEPTIONS

You add -s, not -es, to the following words to form the plural.

cuckoo   kangaroo   patio   piano   ratio   studio
tobacco

EXERCISE

■ Write out the singular and plural of the above exceptions in your workbook *three times*.

■ Learn them off by heart.

■ With a partner, test each other's knowledge of these exceptions to the rule.

EITHER/OR

The following words can add either -s or -es to form the plural, but just -s is the most usual.

fresco	frescos/frescoes
memento	mementos/mementoes
salvo	salvos/salvoes

b

RULE

Words ending in -s add -es to form the plural.

EXAMPLE

Singular			*Plural*
address	+ es	=	addresses
▲	▲		
ends in -s	add -es		

EITHER/OR

The following words ending in -us can either add -es to the singular or replace -us with -i to form the plural. You can choose either of these forms, but -es is becoming more common.

cactus	cactuses/cacti
octopus	octopuses/octopi
syllabus	syllabuses/syllabi
terminus	terminuses/termini

EXERCISE

■ Write out the plurals of the following words using the above rule.

address   bus   business   class   empress   goddess
mass   sorceress walrus

c

RULE

Words ending in -x add -es to the singular to form the plural.

EXAMPLE

box   + es   =   box<u>es</u>

▲   ▲
ends in -x   add -es

EXERCISE

■ Write out the following list of commonly used words ending in -x *three times* in your workbook.

box	boxes
climax	climaxes
fox	foxes
hoax	hoaxes
tax	taxes

14

d

RULE

Words ending in **-ch** or **-sh** add **-es** to the singular to form the plural.

EXAMPLE

| match | + es | = | matches |

ends in **-ch**   add **-es**

EXERCISE

■ Add **-es** to the following words to form plurals.

belch	bleach	coach	church	crash	flash
gash	inch	lash	patch	parish	torch
search	watch				

3 WORDS ENDING IN '-Y'

a

RULE

Words ending in **-y** *after a consonant* change the **-y** to **-i** before adding **-es**.

EXAMPLE

| agony | + s | = | agonies |

ends in **-y**   change **-y** to **-i**
after a   and add **-es**
consonant

EXERCISE

■ Turn the following singulars into plurals using the above rule.

agony	baby	body	century	company	copy
country	dairy	diary	fly	lily	melody
nursery	story	victory			

b

RULE

Words ending in -y *after a vowel* keep the -y and add -s.

EXAMPLE

boy	+ s	=	boys
▲			▲
ends in -y			add -s
after a vowel			

EXERCISE

■ Write out the singular and plural of the following words in your workbook using the above rule.

boy	donkey	key	monkey	play	quay
tray	toy				

4

RULE

Words ending in -f or -fe usually change the -f or -fe to -ve before adding -s.

EXAMPLES

calf	+ s	=	calves
▲			▲
ends in -f			change -f to -ve
			and add -s

life	+ s	=	lives
▲			▲
ends in -fe			change -fe to -ve
			and add -s

EXERCISE

■ Write out the singular and plural of the following words in your workbook using the above rule.

calf	half	knife	leaf	life	loaf
sheaf	thief	wife			

EXCEPTIONS

Here is a list of the most common exceptions to the above rule. These words just add -s to make the plural.

belief	chief	grief	proof	roof

EXERCISES

■ Write out the singular and plural of the exceptions given above in your workbook.

■ Learn the list off by heart.

EITHER/OR

The following words can either just add -s to the singular or change the -f to -ve before adding -s to form the plural.

dwarf	dwarfs/dwarves
scarf	scarfs/scarves
hoof	hoofs/hooves

5 **UNUSUAL PLURALS**

a **RULE**

In words ending in -is you change the -is to -es to form the plural.

EXAMPLE

basis   *becomes*   bases
▲   ▲
ends in -is   change -is to -es

EXERCISE

■ Write out the singular and plural of the following words in your workbook using the above rule.

basis   crisis   diagnosis   emphasis   oasis   thesis

b **RULE**

Words ending in -um usually change the -um to -a to form the plural.

EXAMPLE

stratum   *becomes*   strata
▲   ▲
ends in -um   change -um to -a

Often the modern practice with these words is simply to add -s to the singular to form the plural.

Here is a list of the more common words like this with the alternative included where appropriate. Either form may be used.

bacterium	bacteria
emporium	emporia/emporiums
maximum	maxima/maximums
medium	media/mediums
minimum	minima/minimums
spectrum	spectra
stadium	stadia/stadiums
stratum	strata

c

RULE

A number of specialised words ending in -us change the -us to -i to form the plural. In each case modern practice allows you to add -es to the -us to form an alternative plural.

EXAMPLES

Here are the most common of these words.

cactus	cacti/cactuses
fungus	fungi/funguses
gladiolus	gladioli/gladioluses
radius	radii/radiuses

d

RULE

Some words ending in -a change the -a to -ae to form the plural. Modern practice allows you just to add -s to the singular as an alternative in forming the plural.

EXAMPLES

formula	formulae/formulas
pupa	pupae/pupas

e

RULE

In words from French ending in -eau you normally add -x to the singular to form the plural. Modern practice allows you to add -s to the -eau as an alternative.

EXAMPLES

château	châteaux/châteaus
gateau	gateaux/gateaus
plateau	plateaux/plateaus

18

f

RULE

A number of words change their spelling in the plural. They are all words which you may use a lot.

EXAMPLES

Here is a list of the main ones.

Singular	Plural
child	children
foot	feet
goose	geese
louse	lice
man	men
mouse	mice
ox	oxen
tooth	teeth
woman	women

EXERCISE

■ Write out each word from the above list *three times* in your workbook.

g

RULE

Some words stay the same in the singular and the plural.

EXAMPLES

Here is a list of the most common words like this.

Singular	Plural
deer	deer
fish	fish/fishes
reindeer	reindeer/reindeers
rendezvous	rendezvous
salmon	salmon
sheep	sheep
species	species

h

RULE

To form the plural of some *compound words* you add -s to the *first* word.

EXAMPLES

Here is a list of words like this.

Singular	*Plural*
brother-in-law	brothers-in-law
father-in-law	fathers-in-law
mother-in-law	mothers-in-law
sister-in-law	sisters-in-law
court martial	courts martial

19

UNIT REVIEW EXERCISES

■ Make a list of singulars and plurals of the words in the list below, just like in the example given. Remember to *keep checking* with all the rules and exceptions given in this Unit while you do this exercise.

marshmallow	label	kiss	home	fox	library
monkey	toy	latch	star	hatch	scorpion
potato	climax	boy	girl	penknife	sheep
woman	child				

EXAMPLE

Singular	*Plural*
stamp	stamps

■ Make a list of singulars and plurals of the following words as in the previous exercise.

box	story	bus	thief	crisis	tray
diary	match	oasis	goose	brother-in-law	piano
coach	goddess	body	wife	tobacco	business
mouse	salmon	chief	kangaroo	play	lily

SENTENCE MAKERS

■ Make up a sentence of your own for each of the following words. Try to make your sentences interesting or funny.

address	loaves	boys	crashes	octopuses	melodies
dwarfs	toys	gladioli	oxen	deer	classes
tomatoes	potatoes	thieves	monkeys	businesses	oases
geese					

■ Make up *three* sentences of your own, each of which uses *two or more* of the above words.

PART 2

Vowels and Vowel Clusters

1 **IE/EI**

Words containing '-ie-' or '-ei-'

Knowing when to spell words with -ie- or -ei- causes many people a real problem. Yet this needn't be so. There are not as many -ie-/-ei- root words in English as you would imagine. The rules for using -ie-/-ei- are clear and have very few exceptions. You can in the course of this Unit learn all the most important -ie-/-ei- words and you need not make a mistake with these words again.

RULE

'i' comes before 'e', except after 'c', when the sound is 'ee' as in 'key' or 'bee'.

When the sound is *not* 'ee', then the 'e' normally comes before the 'i'.

a RULE

The sound is 'ee' and does *not* follow 'c', so the 'i' normally comes before the 'e'.

The main words like this are:

achieve	believe	brief	chief	diesel	field
fiend	fierce	grief	niece	piece	pierce
priest	relieve	shield	siege	thief	wield
yield					

EXERCISES

■ Write out the above words *three times* each in your workbook.

■ Learn the list off by heart.

■ With a partner, test each other on these words.

EXCEPTIONS

protein   seize   weir   weird

b

RULE

The sound is 'ee' and follows 'c', so the 'e' comes before the 'i'.

The main words like this are:

ceiling   conceit   conceive   deceit   deceive   perceive   **21**
receipt   receive

There are no exceptions to this.

EXERCISES

■ Write out the above words *three times* each.

■ Learn the list off by heart.

■ With a partner, test each other on these words.

c

RULE

When the sound is *not* 'ee', then 'e' comes before 'i'.

The main words like this are:

eight   feint   foreign   height   heir   leisure
neigh   neighbour   reign   sleigh   their   veil
vein   weight

EXCEPTIONS

friend   view

EXERCISES

■ Write out the above lists of words for the rule and the
exceptions *three times* each.

■ Learn the above lists off by heart.

■ With a partner, test each other on these words.

d

NOTE

There are some words which have -ie- in them which are different from the ones above. These words do not have one syllable but *two*. You pronounce the 'i' and the 'e' separately. They do not follow the above rules. The 'i' always comes before the 'e'.

EXAMPLES

'diet'   pronounced   'di - et'
'anxiety'   pronounced   'anxi -ety'

Important words like this are:

alien   anxiety   audience   client   conscience   diet
fiery   lenient   notoriety   orient   society   soldier
variety

EXERCISES

■ Write out each word from the above list *three* times.

■ Repeat these words over to yourself so you can hear the two syllables.

■ With a partner, test yourself on these words.

UNIT REVIEW EXERCISES

■ Here is a list of words involving -ie-/-ei-. Write out *why* they are spelt the way they are. Do this as shown in the examples given below.

chief   vein   height   niece   receive   fierce
seize   their   ceiling   eight   friend   conceit
piece   neighbour   pierce

EXAMPLES

priest is -ie- because the sound is 'ee' and does not follow 'c'.
perceive is -ei- because the sound is 'ee' and follows 'c'.
foreign is -ei- because the sound is *not* 'ee'.
weird has the sound 'ee' but is an exception.
view does *not* have the sound 'ee' but is an exception.

■ Write out *two* sentences: *one* using the word **either** and *one* using the word **neither**.

SENTENCE MAKERS

■ For each of the words listed below, write a sentence of your own. Try to make your sentences interesting or funny.

brief	sleigh	priest	conscience	their	leisure
weight	reign	heir	shield	thief	deceive
ceiling	yield	believed			

23

■ Make up *three* sentences of your own, each using *two or more* of the words from the above list.

2 EA

Words containing '-ea-'

There are a large number of words with -ea- in them. Here is a useful list of the most common words with -ea- in them.

appear	beach	bear *(to carry; animal)*	beast		beautiful
beneath	bread	breath	cease	cheap	conceal
cream	creature	death	defeat	dream	earth
easy	fear	feather	grease	great	heart
heaven	heavy	increase	jealous	leaf	learn
least	leave	meadow	meanwhile	measure	please
pleasure	reach	ready	really	reason	season
spread	squeal	stream	thread	threat	treasure
wealth	weapon	weather	year		

EXERCISES

■ Write out each word from the above list in your workbook.

■ Make up a sentence of your own for each of the words in the list below.

appeared	beautiful	beneath	heavily	meanwhile	thread
weather	concealed	greatly	defeat	please	squealed
screaming	easily	breathed			

■ Make up *three* sentences, each using *two or more* words from the list in the above exercise.

3 EE

Words containing '-ee-'

a

Here is a useful list of words which end in -ee.

agree	bootee	degree	employee	flee	free
glee	matinée	purée	referee	tree	

b

Here is a useful list of words which have -ee- in them.

beech *(tree)*	beef	beetle	breeze	career	cheerio
cheese	creed	deed	deep	deer *(animal)*	exceed
feeble	freeze	geese	greet	leek *(vegetable)*	
needle	peep	queer	screech	sleeve	sneeze
squeeze	succeed	three	wheel	wheeze	

4

EXERCISES

■ Write out each word from the above lists of words containing -ee- in your workbook.

■ Make up a sentence of your own for each of the words in the list below.

agreed	beer	weeds	peeping	meekly	sleek
speech	succeed	needed	queen	sneered	veered
freely	cheetah	feelings			

■ Make up *three* sentences, each using *two or more* words from the list in the above exercise.

4

UI

Words containing '-ui-'

There are *not* many words with -ui- in them but they can cause people problems. Here is a list of the most common words with -ui-.

biscuit	bruise	build	circuit	fluid	fortuitous
fruit	guide	guilt	juice	nuisance	penguin
recruit	ruin	sluice	suicide	suit	suite
tuition					

EXERCISES

■ Write out each word from the above list *three* times in your workbook.

■ Learn the list off by heart.

■ With a partner test each other's knowledge of these words.

■ For each of the words in the list below, write a sentence of your own. Try to make your sentences interesting or funny.

penguins	recruited	juicy	biscuit	building	guilty
nuisances	bruised	ruined	suite	suit	tuition
fluids				

■ Make up *three* sentences of your own, each using *two or more* of the words from the list in the above exercise.

5 OU

Words containing '-ou-'

There are many words with -ou- in them. Often they are part of a larger cluster, for example, -ough, -our or -ous.

a WORDS CONTAINING -OU-

Here is a useful list of words with -ou- in them.

account	could	couldn't	council	count	countess
couple	coupon	double	doubt	ground	group
house	mountain	mouse	noun	nourishment	ounce
pounce	pound	rouge	round	route	scoundrel
scout	scrounge	should	shouldn't	shoulder	shout
soul	sound	soup	souvenir	stout	thousand
tour	trouble	would	wouldn't	wound	youth

EXERCISES

■ Write out each word from the above list in your workbook.

■ Add the endings -ed and -ing to the following words as in the examples given below.

count   doubt   group   pound   shout   sound
tour   wound *(hurt)*

EXAMPLES

	-ed	-ing
account	accounted	accounting
pounce	pounced	pouncing

■ Make up a sentence of your own using each of the words in the list below.

accountant	councillor	should	wouldn't
shouldered	mountain	aroused	cousins
troublemaker	groups	shouting	ounces
would	doubled	wounding	souvenirs
touring	could	youthful	couple

■ Make up *three* sentences, each using *two or more* of the words from the list in the above exercise.

b ### WORDS ENDING IN -OUGH

Here is a list of the most frequently used words ending in **-ough**.

although	bough	cough	dough	enough	plough
rough	thorough	though	through	tough	trough

6

EXERCISES

- Write out each word from the above list *three* times in your workbook.
- Learn the list off by heart.
- With a partner, test each other's knowledge of this list.
- Make up a sentence of your own for each of the following words. Try to make your sentences interesting or funny.

although	coughing	though	enough	thoroughly
ploughman	roughest	through	tougher	

- Make up *three* sentences, each using *two or more* of the words from the list in the above exercise.

c ### WORDS CONTAINING -OUGHT-

Here is a list of the most frequently used words with **-ought-** in them.

bought	brought	drought	fought	ought	sought
thought	thoughtful	thoughtless			

EXERCISES

- Write out each word from the above list *three* times in your workbook.
- Learn this list off by heart.
- With a partner, test each other's knowledge of this list.
- Make up a sentence of your own for each of the words in the above list.

d WORDS CONTAINING -OUR-

Here is a useful list of words with -our- in them.

colour	courage	course	courteous	endeavour	favourite
flavour	flour	four	fourteen	glamour	honour
hour	journey	mournful	our	ourselves	pour
rumour	scour	sour	splendour	valour	vapour
vigour	your	yourselves			

EXERCISES

- Write out each word from the above list in your workbook.
- Make up a sentence of your own for each of the following words.

floury   journeys   ourselves   courteously   fourteen   mournful
courageous   hours   pouring   rumours   favourite
endeavoured   colouring   your

- Make up *three* sentences, each using *two or more* words from the list in the above exercise.

e WORDS ENDING IN -IOUR

There are very few words in common use which end in -iour.

behaviour   misbehaviour   saviour

EXERCISES

- Write out the above words *twice* in your workbook.
- Make up a sentence of your own for each of the above words.

f WORDS ENDING IN -OUS

Here is a useful list of words which end in -ous.

dangerous	enormous	fabulous	famous	generous
glamorous	humorous	jealous	marvellous	nervous
numerous	perilous	prosperous	ravenous	ridiculous
rigorous	ruinous	treacherous	tremendous	unanimous
vigorous				

EXERCISES

- Write out each word from the above list in your workbook.
- Make up a sentence of your own for each of the following words.

dangerously   enormous   glamorous   nervous   jealously
vigorous   perilously   treacherous   rigorously   tremendous
unanimous   generously   marvellous   numerous   famous

g WORDS ENDING IN -IOUS

Here is a useful list of words which end in **-ious**.

anxious	cautious	conscious	curious	delicious	envious
glorious	gracious	harmonious	hilarious	industrious	infectious
mysterious	obvious	precarious	rebellious	religious	studious
tenacious	various	vicious	victorious		

EXERCISES

■ Write out each word from the above list in your workbook.

■ For each of the following words, make up a sentence of your own.

anxiously	glorious	hilarious	infectious	cautious
mysteriously	consciously	harmonious	tenaciously	envious
obviously	delicious	industrious	rebellious	graciously
religious	various	viciously		

h WORDS ENDING IN -EOUS

Here is a useful list of words which end in **-eous**.

advantageous	beauteous	courageous	courteous
erroneous	gaseous	gorgeous	herbaceous
hideous	igneous	instantaneous	miscellaneous
outrageous	piteous	plenteous	righteous
simultaneous			

EXERCISES

■ Write out each word from the above list in your workbook.

■ For each of the following words, make up a sentence of your own.

courageous	outrageous	simultaneously	courteous
hideous	gorgeous		

i WORDS ENDING IN -UOUS

Here is a useful list of words which end in **-uous**.

ambiguous	arduous	conspicuous	continuous	impetuous
incongruous	innocuous	sensuous	strenuous	sumptuous
superfluous	tumultuous	voluptuous		

EXERCISES

- Write out each word from the above list *twice* in your workbook.
- For each of the following words, make up a sentence of your own.

conspicuously   strenuous   voluptuous   innocuous
continuously   ambiguous

6 AU

Words containing '-au-'

There are a large number of words with -au- in them, sometimes as part of a larger cluster, for example, -augh- and -aught-.

a WORDS CONTAINING -AU-

Here is a useful list of commonly used words which have the cluster -au- in them.

applause	assault	auburn	auction	August
aunt	author	automatic	autumn	beauty
because	cauldron	cauliflower	cause	caution
chauffeur	daub	exhaust	fault	fraud
gauge	gaunt	gauze	haul	haunt
launch	laundry	laurel	maul	mauve
nausea	pause	restaurant	saucer	saunter
sausage	taunt			

EXERCISES

- Write out each word from the above list *twice* in your workbook.
- Make up interesting or funny sentences of your own using the following words.

applauding   restaurant   caution   author   caused
haunted   because   autumn   beautiful   sausages
gauges   auburn   chauffeur   paused

- Make up *three* sentences, each using *two or more* of the words from the list in the above exercise.

b WORDS CONTAINING -AUGH-/-AUGHT-

Here is a useful list of words containing -augh- or -aught-.

caught   daughter draught   laugh   laughter naughty
slaughter taught

30

EXERCISES

■ Write out each word from the above list *three times* in your workbook.

■ For each of the following words, make up a sentence of your own.

laughed caught naughty slaughtered taught daughter

7 # EU

Words containing '-eu-'

Words with -eu- in them are mainly words of foreign derivation. Here is a useful list of such words.

amateur deuce   feud   lieutenant milieu   neuralgia
neuter   neutral pasteurise pneumatic rheumatism sleuth

EXERCISES

■ Write out each word from the above list *twice* in your workbook.

■ Choose *three* of the above words and use each one in a sentence.

8 # UA

Words containing '-ua-'

Here is a useful list of words with -ua- in them.

actual   casual   factual   gradual   graduate guard
truant   valuable virtual   visual   usual

EXERCISES

■ Write out this list *twice* in your workbook.

■ For each of the following words, make up a sentence of your own.

actually casual usually gradually guards truant

9 | EO

Words containing '-eo-'

Here is a useful list of words containing the -eo- cluster.

cameo	chameleon	dungeon	galleon	leopard	leotard
meteorite	neon	people	pigeon	surgeon	truncheon
video					

EXERCISES

■ Write out each word from the above list *twice* in your workbook.

■ For each of the following words, make up a sentence of your own.

leotard   pigeons   dungeon   people   video   leopards

PART 3

Doubling the Final Consonant

When you add an ending or suffix to a word ending in a single vowel, sometimes you *double* the final consonant and sometimes you *don't*. Knowing when to do this and when not to is a worry for many people in their writing. BUT IT NEEDN'T BE!

The rules for doubling or not doubling the final consonant are really quite straightforward and have very few exceptions. Through the exercises you will soon master these rules and enjoy the confidence in your writing which flows from this.

1

P

Words ending in '-p'

WHEN YOU <u>DOUBLE</u> THE '-P':

a

RULE

You double the final -p in one-syllable words which have a single vowel before the -p when followed by an ending or suffix beginning with a vowel.

EXAMPLE

chop   + ed   =   chopped

▲   ▲   ▲

one syllable,   vowel   double the -p

single vowel

EXERCISES

■ Add -ed to the following words using the above rule.

lap	skip	flap	strip	drip	snap
trap	cap	pop	mop		

■ Add -ing to the following words using the above rule.

dip	map	sip	drop	rip	step
tap	lop	shop	top		

■ Add -er to the following words using the above rule.

trip	dip	stop	shop	slip

b

RULE

You *double* the final -p in words of *more than one* syllable when the stress falls on the final syllable.

EXAMPLE

equip	+ ed	=	equipped
▲	▲		▲
stress falls on final syllable	vowel		double the -p

EXERCISE

■ Write the following words out *three times* in your workbook.

equip   equipped   equipping

WHEN YOU DO NOT DOUBLE THE '-P':

a

RULE

You *don't* double the final -p when adding an ending beginning with a vowel if there are *two* vowels immediately before the -p.

EXAMPLE

keep	+ er	=	keeper
▲	▲		▲
two vowels	vowel		single -p

EXERCISES

■ Add -ed to the following words using the above rule.

bleep   droop   loop   reap   scoop   soap
stoop   swoop

■ Add -ing to the following words.

creep   droop   heap   keep   peep   sleep
snoop   sweep

■ Add -er to the following words.

creep   keep   reap   snoop

b

RULE

You *don't* double the final -p in words of *more than one* syllable ending in a single vowel before the -p if the stress *does not* fall on the final syllable.

There are only *three* commonly used words like this. These are:

develop	gallop	hiccup

EXAMPLE

develop	+ ed	=	developed
stress on earlier syllable	vowel		single -p

TABLE

develop	developed	developing	developer
gallop	galloped	galloping	
hiccup	hiccuped	hiccuping	

EXCEPTION

Note that **kidnap** is an exception. Here the stress *does not* fall on the last syllable but you double the -p.

kidnap	kidnapped	kidnapping	kidnapper

EXERCISES

■ Write out the above table and the exception *three* times in your workbook.

■ Learn them all by heart.

■ With a partner, test each other's knowledge of these words.

UNIT REVIEW EXERCISE

■ Add -ed, -ing and -er where you can to the words in the list below, just like in the example given. Watch for those words which double the -p and those which don't!

Not all words will have an entry in each column.

chop	reap	crop	loop	hiccup	drop
develop	soap	gallop	kidnap	stoop	group
rip	shop	troop			

EXAMPLE

	-ed	-ing	-er
wrap	wrapped	wrapping	wrapper

SENTENCE MAKERS

■ Make up a sentence of your own for each of the following words.
Try to make your sentences interesting or funny.

| stopped | supper | developed | steering | galloping | dropped |
| group | kidnapper | keeping | hiccuped | sleeping | swooped |

■ Make up *three* sentences of your own, each using *two or more* words
from the above list.

2 R

Words ending in '-r' after a vowel

WHEN YOU <u>DOUBLE</u> THE FINAL '-R':

a

RULE

You *double* the final -r in one-syllable words which have a single
vowel before the -r when followed by an ending or suffix beginning
with a vowel.

EXAMPLE

| bar | + ed | = | barred |

▲ | ▲ | | ▬

one syllable, vowel double the -r
single vowel

EXERCISES

■ Add -ed and -ing to the following words using the above rule.
Do it just like in the example given.

| blur | char | jar | mar | scar | slur |
| spur | star | stir | tar | | |

EXAMPLE

| | -ed | -ing |
| bar | barred | barring |

b

RULE

You also *double* the final -r in words of *more than one* syllable when there is a single vowel before the -r and the stress falls on the final syllable.

EXAMPLE

refer   + ed   =   referred

stress on final   vowel   double the -r
syllable

EXERCISES

■ Add -ed to the following words using the above rule.

concur   defer   incur   inter *(bury)*   recur

■ Add -ing to the following words.

confer   deter   infer   prefer   transfer

WHEN YOU DO NOT DOUBLE THE '-R':

a

RULE

You *don't* double the final -r before a following vowel when there are *two* vowels before the -r.

EXAMPLES

near   + ing   =   nearing

two vowels   vowel   don't double the -r

appear   + ance   appearance

EXERCISES

■ Add -ed to the following words using the above rule.

appear   clear   devour   jeer   pair   pour   rear   sneer

■ Add -ing to the following words.

despair   fear   moor   peer   roar   tear   tour   wear

■ Add -er to the following words.

bear   clear   hear   pour   scour   wear

b

RULE

You *don't* double the final -r in words ending in a single vowel before the -r if the stress *does not* fall on the final syllable.

EXAMPLE

enter + ed = entered

stress on earlier   vowel   don't double the -r
syllable

3·

EXERCISES

■ Add -ed to the following words using the above rule.

| answer | border | cluster | cover | hammer | linger |
| offer | pester | scatter | thunder | | |

■ Add -ing to the following words.

| batter | cater | chatter | conquer | consider | encounter |
| gather | hover | order | prosper | utter | whimper |

UNIT REVIEW EXERCISE

■ Add -ed and -ing to the following words just like in the examples given. Remember some words double the -r and some don't.

blur	concur	cater	spur	transfer	stir
tar	answer	cover	refer	peer	prefer
scar	roar	gather	moor	consider	

EXAMPLES

	-ed	*-ing*
star	starred	starring
pour	poured	pouring

SENTENCE MAKERS

■ Make up a sentence of your own for each of the following words. Try to make your sentences interesting or funny.

| stirred | transferring | appearance | roared | wearing |
| pestered | scattering | covered | jeering | |

■ Make up *three* sentences of your own, each using *two or more* words from the above list.

3

N

Words ending in '-n' after a vowel

WHEN YOU <u>DOUBLE</u> THE '-N':

a

RULE

You *double* the final -n in one-syllable words which have a single vowel before the -n when followed by an ending or suffix beginning with a vowel.

EXAMPLE

run	+ er	=	runner
▲	▲		▲
one syllable, single vowel	vowel		double the -n

EXERCISES

■ Add **-ed** to the following words using the above rule.

| can | fan | grin | gun | scan | sin | stun |

■ Add **-ing** to the following words.

| ban | grin | pin | plan | run | sin | spin |

---

b

RULE

You also double the final -n in words of *more than one* syllable when there is a single vowel before the -n and the stress falls on the final syllable.

EXAMPLES

begin	+ er	=	beginner
▲	▲		▲
stress on final syllable	vowel		double the -n

| begin | + ing | = | beginning |

WHEN YOU <u>DO NOT</u> DOUBLE THE '-N':

a

RULE

You *don't* double the final -n before a following vowel when there are two vowels before the -n.

EXAMPLE

lean	+ ing	=	leaning
▲	▲		▲
two vowels	vowel		don't double the -n

EXERCISES

■ Add -ed to the following words using the above rule.

bargain   chain   detain   groan   moan   obtain
refrain   stain

■ Add -ing to the following words.

captain   contain   gain   join   preen   rain
train

■ Add -er to the following words.

contain   join   moan   train

b

RULE

You *don't* double the final -n in words ending in a single vowel before the -n if the stress *does not* fall on the final syllable.

EXAMPLE

garden	+ er	=	gardener
▲	▲		▲
stress on earlier syllable	vowel		don't double the -n

EXERCISES

■ Add -ed to the following words using the above rule.

awaken   brighten   harden   iron   orphan   straighten
thicken   toughen

■ Add -ing to the following words.

brighten   garden   jettison   reason   sweeten   tighten

UNIT REVIEW EXERCISE

■ Add **-ed**, **-ing** and **-er**, where you can, to the following words just like in the example given. Remember some words double the **-n** and others don't! Remember also that not all words will take each ending.

lean	scan	train	begin	sin	harden
join	maintain	spin	garden	rain	straighten
open	run				

EXAMPLE

	-ed	*-ing*	*-er*
stun	stunned	stunning	————
contain	contained	containing	container

SENTENCE MAKERS

■ Make up a sentence of your own for each of the following words. Try to make your sentences interesting or funny.

| runners | stunning | sweeteners | gained | obtaining | container |
| spinning | pinned | gardening | gunned | | |

■ Make up *three* sentences of your own, each using *two or more* words from the above list.

4   T

Words ending in '-t' after a vowel

> WHEN YOU <u>DOUBLE</u> THE '-T':

a   RULE

You *double* the final **-t** in one-syllable words which have a single vowel before the **-t** when followed by an ending or suffix beginning with a vowel.

EXAMPLE

cut	+ ing	=	cutting
▲	▲		▲
one syllable, single vowel	vowel		double the **-t**

EXERCISES

■ Add **-ed** to the following words using the above rule.

bat   chat   dot   jet   knit   knot   spot   trot

■ Add **-ing** to the following words.

bet   fret   knit   let   pat   put   quit   sit   spot   trot

41

b

RULE

You also *double* the final **-t** before a following vowel in words of *more than one* syllable if there is a single vowel before the **-t** and the stress falls upon the final syllable.

EXAMPLE

commit   + ed   =   committed

stress on final   double the **-t**
syllable, single
vowel before **-t**

EXERCISES

■ Add **-ed** to the following words using the above rule.

commit   outwit   regret   remit   submit

■ Add **-ing** to the following words.

babysit   commit   forget   outwit   regret   remit   submit

WHEN YOU DO NOT DOUBLE THE '-T':

---

a

RULE

You *don't* double the final **-t** before a following vowel when there are *two* vowels before the **-t**.

EXAMPLE

seat   + ed   =   seated

two vowels   single **-t**

EXERCISES

■ Add **-ed** to the following words using the above rule.

defeat   entreat   float   heat   riot   spout   sprout   treat

■ Add **-ing** to the following words.

coat   eat   float   meet   riot   seat   spout   treat

b

RULE

You *don't* double the final -t before a following vowel in words ending in a single vowel before the -t if the stress *does not* fall on the final syllable.

42

EXAMPLE

profit   + ed   =   profited

▲   ▲   ▲

stress on earlier   vowel   single -t
syllable, single
vowel before -t

EXERCISES

■ Add **-ed** to the following words using the above rule.

ballot   benefit   budget   credit   deposit   exhibit
limit   market   profit   prohibit rocket   target

■ Add **-ing** to the following words.

benefit   budget   carpet   credit   deposit   edit
exhibit   market   plummet   profit   rocket   target
visit

EXCEPTION

outfit   outfitted   outfitting

▲

stress on
earlier syllable

Here the stress *does not* fall on the final syllable but you still double the -t.

UNIT REVIEW EXERCISE

■ Add **-ed**, **-ing** and **-er** where you can to the following words just as in the examples given. Remember, some words double the -t and some don't! Not all words will take each ending.

dot   commit   limit   heat   fret   defeat   prohibit
knit   benefit   trot   outfit   outwit   pat   treat
market   seat   credit   submit

EXAMPLE

	-ed	*-ing*	*-er*
riot	rioted	rioting	rioter
jet	jetted	jetting	——

SENTENCE MAKERS

■ Make up a sentence of your own for each of the following words.
Try to make your sentences interesting or funny.

battling   chatted   forgetting committee defeated treating
prohibited targeting visited   seating   visitor   floated

■ Make up *three* sentences of your own, each using *two or more* words
from the above list.

5 L

Words ending in '-l' after a vowel

WHEN YOU DOUBLE THE '-L':

RULE

You double the final -l after a single vowel and before an ending or
suffix beginning with a vowel *no matter where the stress falls* in the
root word.

EXAMPLES

patrol	+ ed	=	patrolled
stress on final syllable	vowel		double the -l

grovel	+ ing	=	grovelling
stress on earlier syllable	vowel		double the -l

EXERCISES

■ Add **-ed** to the following words using the above rule.

cancel   control equal   jewel   label model
parcel   propel   rival   tunnel

■ Add **-ing** to the following words.

appal   compel distil   excel   level panel
pencil repel   signal   travel

WHEN YOU <u>DO NOT</u> DOUBLE THE '-L':

RULE

You *don't* double the final -l before a following vowel when there are two vowels before the -l.

EXAMPLE

appeal ′ + ed = appealed

two vowels   single -l

EXCEPTION

The word **dial** has *two* vowels before the final -l, but you *double* the -l.

dial   dialled   dialling

EXERCISES

■ Add -ed to the following words using the above rule.

| bail | conceal | dial | fail | hail | heal |
| oil | retail | veil | wheel | | |

■ Add -ing to the following words.

| boil | cool | deal | detail | fool | kneel |
| mail | pool | reveal | toil | | |

UNIT REVIEW EXERCISE

■ Add -ed, -ing and -er, where you can, to the following words just as in the examples given. Remember, some words double the -l and some don't! Not all words will have an entry in each column.

cancel	oil	fail	equal	veil	propel	wheel
travel	appeal	signal	grovel	reveal	tunnel	dial
label	excel	compel	cool			

EXAMPLES

	-ed	*-ing*	*-er*
boil	boiled	boiling	boiler
pencil	pencilled	pencilling	___

SENTENCE MAKERS

■ Make up a sentence of your own for each of the following words.

aimed appalling appealed modelling excellent compelled
jewellery revealed feeling boiled equalled signalling

■ Make up *three* sentences of your own, each using *two or more* words from the above list.

44

6 | M

Words ending in '-m' after a vowel

WHEN YOU DOUBLE THE '-M':

RULE

You *double* the final -m in one-syllable words which have a single vowel before the -m when followed by an ending or suffix beginning with a vowel.

EXAMPLE

dim	+ ed	=	dimmed
▲	▲		▲
one syllable, single vowel	vowel		double the -m

EXERCISES

■ Add -ed to the following words using the above rule.

dim   hum   ram   rim   skim   slim   trim

■ Add -ing to the following words.

cram   drum   ram   slim   stem   strum   swim   trim

WHEN YOU DO NOT DOUBLE THE '-M':

a

RULE

You *don't* double the final -m before a following vowel when there are *two* vowels before the -m.

EXAMPLE

cream	+ ed	=	creamed
▲	▲		▲
two vowels	vowel		single -m

EXERCISES

■ Add -ed to the following words using the above rule.

aim bloom dream groom redeem scream seem team

■ Add -ing to the following words.

aim beam dream gleam maim room seem zoom

b

RULE

You *don't* double the final -m in words ending in a *single* vowel before the -m if the stress *does not* fall on the final syllable.

EXAMPLE

blossom   + ed   =   blossomed
▲   ▲   ▲
stress on   vowel   single -m
on earlier syllable

EXERCISES

■ Here is a list of the most common words fitting the above rule. Write them out in your workbook as they are given below.

blossom   blossomed   blossoming
custom   customer
ransom   ransomed   ransoming
venom   venomous

■ Learn them off by heart.

■ With a partner, test each other's knowledge of this small list.

UNIT REVIEW EXERCISE

■ Add -ed, -ing and -er, where you can, to the following words just as in the examples given. Remember some words double the -m and some don't! Not all words will have an entry in each column.

dim   bloom   hum   redeem   skim   scream
drum   blossom   ransom   swim   aim   slim
seem   custom   stem   trim

EXAMPLES

	-ed	*-ing*	*-er*
gleam	gleamed	gleaming	——
dream	dreamed	dreaming	dreamer

SENTENCE MAKERS

■ Make up a sentence of your own for each of the following words. Try to make your sentences interesting or funny.

dimmed   redeemed   drumming   screaming   slimmer   seemed
swimming dreaming   zoomed   hummed

■ Make up *three* sentences of your own, each using *two or more* words from the above list.

7 | B

Words ending in '-b' after a vowel

RULE

You always *double* the final -b if it follows a vowel and is before an ending or suffix beginning with a vowel.

EXAMPLE

rib	+ ed	=	ribbed
▲	▲		▬
-b follows a vowel	vowel		double the -b

EXERCISES

■ Add **-ed** to the following words using the above rule.

bob   dab   jab   lob   rob   scrub   swab   throb

■ Add **-ing** to the following words.

club   fib   grab   rub   stab   scrub   swab   throb

■ Add **-er** to the following words.

fib   rob   rub   scrub

SENTENCE MAKERS

■ Make up a sentence of your own for each of the following words. Try to make your sentences interesting or funny.

bobbed   rubbing   fibber   dabbing   stabbed   throbbing
clubbed   grabbing   robber

■ Make up *three* sentences of your own, each using *two or more* words from the above list.

8 | G

Words ending in '-g' after a vowel

RULE

You *double* the final -g if it follows a vowel and is before an ending or suffix beginning with a vowel.

EXAMPLE

big	+ er	=	bigger
▲	▲		▬
-g follows a vowel	vowel		double the -g

8

EXERCISES

■ Add **-ed** to the following words using the above rule.

bag	brag	drag	flag	gag	jog
nag	sag	slog	wag		

■ Add **-ing** to the following words.

beg	brag	dig	drug	flog	hug
mug	plug	shrug	snag		

■ Add **-er** to the following words.

big	dig	jog	mug

SENTENCE MAKERS

■ Make up a sentence of your own for each of the following words.
Try to make your sentences interesting or funny.

biggest   begging   dragged   mugger   nagging   plugged
shrugging   wagged

■ Make up *three* sentences of your own using *two or more* words from
the above list.

9 S
Words ending in '-s' after a vowel

RULE

There are very few words which end in a single **-s** after a vowel. The
most important ones are listed below. They don't follow a set rule.

EXAMPLES

bus *(noun)*	buses		
bus *(verb)*	bussed	bussing	
gas *(noun)*	gases		
gas *(verb)*	gassed	gassing	
focus *(verb)*	focused	focused	focusing

EXERCISES

■ Write out each word from the above list *three times* in your
workbook.

■ Learn the list off by heart.

■ With a partner, test each other on the list.

SENTENCE MAKERS

■ Make up a sentence of your own for each of the following words.
Try to make your sentences interesting or funny.

buses   gassed   focused   gassing   focusing   gases

10 D

Words ending in '-d' after a vowel

WHEN YOU <u>DOUBLE</u> THE FINAL '-D':

RULE

You *double* the final -d in one-syllable words which have a single
vowel before the -d when followed by an ending or suffix beginning
with a vowel.

EXAMPLE

wed   + ing   =   wedding
▲   ▲   ▲
one syllable,   vowel   double the -d
single vowel

EXERCISES

■ Add -ed to the following words using the above rule.

bed   bud   shred   stud   thud   wed

■ Add -ing to the following words.

bed   bid   gad   shred   thud   wed

■ Add -er to the following words.

bid   red   shred

WHEN YOU <u>DO NOT</u> DOUBLE THE FINAL '-D':

RULE

You *don't* double the final -d before a following vowel when there
are two vowels before the -d.

EXAMPLE

wood   + en   =   wooden
▬   ▲   ▬
two vowels   vowel   single -d

EXERCISES

- Add **-ed** to the following words using the above rule.

  bead dread heed need proceed raid

- Add **-ing** to the following words.

  behead bleed dread exceed head lead
  need proceed

- Add **-er** to the following words.

  feed loud read raid spread

UNIT REVIEW EXERCISE

- Add **-ed**, **-ing** and **-er** where you can to the following words just like in the examples given. Remember some words double the **-d** and some don't! Not all words will take each ending.

  bed behead bid raid stud hood
  thud exceed proceed gag speed thread
  shred read

EXAMPLES

	-ed	-ing	-er
breed	⎯⎯	breeding	breeder
wed	wedded	wedding	⎯⎯

SENTENCE MAKERS

- Make up a sentence of your own for each of the following words. Try to make your sentences interesting or funny.

  needing budded hidden reddest shredding thudded
  redder budding

- Make up *three* sentences of your own, each using *two or more* words from the above list.

11 F

Words ending in '-f' after a vowel

There are very few words which end in a single -**f** after a vowel. All
are words with *two* vowels before the -**f**. You *do not* double the -**f**
before a following vowel in these cases.

5

WORDS

deaf	deafen	
leaf	leafed	leafing
loaf	loafed	loafing
roof	roofed	roofing

EXERCISES

■ Write out each word from the above list *three times* in your
workbook.

■ Learn these words off by heart.

■ With a partner, test each other's knowledge of these words.

SENTENCE MAKERS

■ Make up a sentence of your own for each of the words in the list below.
Try to make your sentences interesting or funny.

deafen   leafed   roofed   loafed   leafing

12 K

Words ending in '-k' after a vowel

WHEN YOU DOUBLE THE '-K':

RULE

You *double* the final -**k** after a single vowel before a following vowel
in words of *one* syllable.

EXAMPLE

There is only one example of this in common use.

trek   + ed   =   trekked
▲   ▲   ▬
single vowel   vowel   double the -k

trek   trekked   trekking

WHEN YOU DO NOT DOUBLE THE '-K':

RULE

You *don't* double the final -k before a following vowel when there are *two* vowels before the -k.

2

EXAMPLE

beak   + ed   =   beaked

two vowels   vowel   single -k

EXERCISES

■ Add -ed to the following words using the above rule.

beak   croak   leak   reek   squeak

■ Add -ing to the following words.

creak   croak   leak   reek   seek   squeak

■ Add -en, -er and -est to the word **weak**.

UNIT REVIEW EXERCISE

■ Add -ed, -ing and -er where you can to the words below just as in the examples given.

creak   leak   reek   seek   squeak   weak

EXAMPLES

	-ed	-ing	-er
beak	beaked	——	beaker
croak	croaked	croaking	——

SENTENCE MAKERS

■ Make up a sentence of your own for each of the following words. Try to make your sentences interesting or funny.

trekking   loafed   weakest   seeking   creaked   squeaking
reeked   trekked   beaker

PART 4

Words Ending in Silent '-e'

There are a large number of words in English which end in a silent -e. A silent -e at the end of a word is an -e that is not pronounced *separately*, though it often affects the pronunciation of the previous vowel.

For example: **write**

Though this *looks* like a word with *two* syllables, it is spoken as *one* syllable. You don't pronounce the -e separately.

RULE

When you add an ending which starts with a vowel to words ending in a silent -e you drop the -e before adding the ending.

EXAMPLES

fame	+ ous	=	famous
▲	▲		▲
silent -e	vowel		you omit the -e
care	+ ing	=	caring

EXERCISES

◼ Add -ing to the following words using the above rule.

capsize	disgrace	erase	injure	like	move
name	place	race	scrape	seize	trade
use	wake	write			

◼ Add -able to the following words.

| advise | cure | desire | imagine | measure | note |
| save | use | value | | | |

EXCEPTIONS

a

Certain words ending in -ge and -ce and followed by -able, -ous or -ance keep the silent -e.

Here are some lists of these words.

Words ending in -ge

change	changeable
knowledge	knowledgeable
manage	manageable
marriage	marriageable
advantage	advantageous
courage	courageous

Words ending in -ce

notice	noticeable
peace	peaceable
service	serviceable
trace	traceable

b Some words ending in silent -e after a vowel keep the -e when followed by -ing.

canoe	canoeing
shoe	shoeing
tiptoe	tiptoeing

c The words **age** and **queue** can either keep the -e or drop it before a following -ing.

age	ageing/aging
queue	queueing/queuing

EXERCISES

■ Write out the lists given in a), b) and c) above *three times* each.

■ Learn these words off by heart.

■ With a partner, test each other on these words.

UNIT REVIEW EXERCISE

■ Add -ing to the following words using the rule and exceptions.

cackle	starve	invite	shoe	gape	tiptoe
note	queue	create	canoe	improve	hide

■ Add -able to the following words.

argue	note	knowledge	desire	excuse	value
notice	cure	peace	change	use	manage

SENTENCE MAKERS

■ For each of the following words, make up a sentence of your own.
Try to make your sentences interesting or funny

carving	noticeable	excusing	famous	courageous
using	placed	capsized	savable	notable
manageable	seizing	imaginable	traced	closing

■ Make up *three* sentences of your own, each using *two or more* words
from the above list.

6

PART 5
Words Ending in '-y'

WORDS ENDING IN '-Y' AFTER A VOWEL

RULE

In words ending in **-y** *after a vowel* the **-y** remains before *all* additional endings.

EXAMPLE

buy   + ing   =   buying

▲   ▲

ends in **-y**   keeps the **-y**

after a
vowel

EXERCISE

■ Add **-ed**, **-er** and **-ing** where you can to the following words just as in the example given. Not all words will have an entry in each column.

employ   enjoy   pay   play   pray   say
stay   stray   toy

EXAMPLE

	-ed	-er	-ing
pray	prayed	prayer	praying

EXCEPTIONS

In certain commonly used words the **-y** after a vowel becomes **-i** before a following consonant.

EXAMPLES

day	+ ly	=	daily
gay	+ ly	=	gaily
pay	+ d	=	paid
say	+ d	=	said

2 WORDS ENDING IN '-Y' AFTER A CONSONANT

a RULE

When you add **-s** or **-d** to a word ending in **-y** after a consonant you change the **-y** to **-ie**.

EXAMPLES

baby	+ s	=	babies

ends in **-y**
after a
consonant

-y becomes **-ie**

dry	+ d	=	dried

EXERCISES

■ In your workbook add **-s** to the following words using the above rule.

agony	dairy	nursery	company	body	fly
certify	copy	deny	identify	satisfy	apply
vary	bakery	grocery	carry	hurry	marry

■ Add **-d** to the following words using the above rule.

| copy | satisfy | bury | reply | worry | supply |
| deny | cry | accompany | vary | hurry | |

b RULE

When you add **-ing** to words ending in **-y** after a consonant you keep the **-y**.

EXAMPLE

deny	+ ing	=	denying

ends in **-y**
after a consonant

keeps the **-y**

EXERCISE

■ Add **-ing** to the following words using the above rule.

| ally | certify | verify | cry | marry | pry |
| defy | apply | purify | supply | bury | carry |

C

RULE

Words ending in **-y** *after a consonant* change the **-y** to an **-i** when an ending is added other than **-s**, **-d** or one beginning with **-i**.

EXAMPLES

beauty	+ ful	=	beautiful
▲	▲		▲
ends in **-y** after a consonant	not **-s**, **-d** or **-i**		**-y** becomes **-i**

easy	+ ly	=	easily

EXERCISES

■ Add **-ly** to the following words using the above rule.

breezy   easy   crazy   ready   noisy   icy
lazy   lucky   busy

■ Add **-er** and **-est** to the following words as in the example below.

bushy   noisy   crazy   silly   lucky   sunny

EXAMPLE

	-er	*-est*
brawny	brawnier	brawniest

■ Add **-ful** to the following words.

duty   mercy   pity   plenty

EXCEPTIONS

In a small number of words ending in **-y** *after a consonant* you change the **-y** to an **-e** before **-ous**.

beauty	+ ous	=	beauteous
pity	+ ous	=	piteous

8

UNIT REVIEW EXERCISES

■ Add **-ing** to the following words.

enjoy   say   supply   carry   hurry   deny
buy   marry

■ Add **-s** and **-d** to the following verbs using the above rules as in the example given.

dry   deny   vary   hurry   apply
accompany   defy   cry   bury   worry

EXAMPLE

	-s	-d
copy	copies	copied

■ Add **-ly** to the following words.

ready   noisy   lucky   busy   easy

SENTENCE MAKERS

■ For each of the following words make up a sentence of your own. Try to make your sentences interesting or funny.

craziest   companies   saying   played   satisfies   drying
replied   babyish   spies   joyful   allies   married
luckily   merciful   easily   beautiful

■ Make up *three* sentences, each using *two or more* words from the above list.

PART 6

Suffixes

1 -ABLE

There are many words which take the suffix -able. Here are the rules for adding -able to a root word.

a RULE

After words ending in a consonant you simply add the suffix.

EXAMPLE

accept   + able   =   acceptable

EXERCISE

■ Add -able to the following words.

approach	attain	avoid	break	comfort	consider
detest	enjoy	fashion	favour	laugh	question
reason	remark	suit			

b RULE

After words ending in a silent -e you drop the -e before adding -able.

EXAMPLE

desire   + able   =   desirable
▲   ▲
silent -e   omit the -e

EXERCISE

■ Add -able to the following words using the above rule.

admire	advise	argue	cure	debate	deplore
excuse	imagine	measure	note	save	use
value					

EITHER/OR

In the following words you can *either* keep the -e *or* omit the -e before -able. The more common usage is given first.

> lovable/loveable
> movable/moveable
> shakeable/shakable

EXCEPTIONS

In words ending in -ge and -ce you keep the -e before -able. Here is a list of the most important words like this.

Words ending in -ge

> changeable
> knowledgeable
> manageable
> marriageable

Words ending in -ce

> peaceable
> serviceable
> traceable

EXERCISE

■ Write out the words in **Either/or** and **Exceptions** above *three times* each in your workbook.

c

RULE

In words ending in -y after a consonant you change the -y to an -i before adding -able.

EXAMPLE

certify   + able   =   certifiable
▲   ▲
ends in -y   change -y to -i
after a
consonant

EXERCISE

■ In your workbook add -able to the following words using the above rule.

> certify   deny   envy   identify   notify   pity
> vary   verify

d **RULE**

In words ending in **-ee** you simply add **-able**.

62

EXAMPLE

agree   + able   =   agreeable

UNIT REVIEW EXERCISE

■ Add **-able** to the following words using the above rules.

change	approach	teach	desire	measure	peace
certify	consider	knowledge	agree	enjoy	break
suit	service	pity	laugh	value	manage
imagine	envy				

SENTENCE MAKERS

■ Make up a sentence of your own for each of the following words. Try to make your sentences interesting or funny.

comfortable	imaginable	pitiable	knowledgeable
favourable	desirable	suitable	notable
agreeable	admirable	variable	remarkable
laughable	changeable	usable	

■ Make up *three* sentences of your own, each using *two or more* words from the above list.

2 # -IBLE

A number of words have **-ible** rather than **-able** at the end of the word. In most of these the **-ible** has become part of, rather than being added to, the root word. You should *learn* these words as there is no particular rule to follow.

WORD LIST

Here is a list of the most important words which end in **-ible**.

accessible	audible	collapsible	combustible	compatible
corruptible	credible	defensible	digestible	divisible
edible	eligible	exhaustible	flexible	forcible
gullible	horrible	illegible	impossible	incredible
intelligible	legible	negligible	perceptible	permissible
plausible	possible	responsible	sensible	terrible

EXERCISES

■ Write out the above word list *twice* in your workbook.

■ Make up a sentence of your own for each of the following words. Try to make your sentences interesting or funny.

audible incredible flexible horrible digestible legible
possible terrible sensible edible responsible permissible

3 FORMING ADVERBS FROM -ABLE/-IBLE WORDS

You form adverbs from **-able** and **-ible** words by changing the final -e to a -y.

EXAMPLES

Adjectives	*Adverb*
impossible	impossibly
suitable	suitably

EXERCISES

■ Make a list in your workbook just like in the examples given of the adjective and adverb forms of the following words.

arguable imaginable notable terrible impossible
favourable comfortable deplorable horrible knowledgeable
laughable forcible agreeable peaceable admirable
responsible remarkable possible

■ For each of the following words, make up a sentence of your own. Try to make your sentences interesting or funny.

terribly agreeably remarkably suitably possible
horribly favourably comfortably

4 –LY

ADDING '-LY' TO AN ADJECTIVE TO FORM AN ADVERB

RULE

In most cases you simply add **-ly** to the adjective to form an adverb whether the adjective ends in a consonant or a vowel.

EXAMPLES

Adjective			*Adverb*
beautiful	+ ly	=	beautifully
sincere	+ ly	=	sincerely

EXERCISES

■ Just like in the examples given above write out a list of the adverbs formed from the following words.

annual	cruel	bright	dangerous	dark
doubtful	exact	harsh	intense	jealous
lame	mature	mortal	needless	outlandish
partial	persistent	rare	savage	secure
sincere	sober	treacherous		

EXCEPTIONS

a

When the adjective ends in -y you change the -y to an -i before adding -ly.

EXAMPLE

Adjective   *Adverb*
busy   + ly   =   busily
▲   ▲
ends in -y   change -y to -i

EXERCISE

■ In your workbook write out the following list and then beside the adjective write out the adverb just like in the example given.

cosy	easy	guilty	hearty	jaunty	lazy
lucky	necessary	noisy	queasy	ready	speedy	tidy

EXAMPLE
Adjective   *Adverb*
busy   busily

b

In the words **true** and **due** you omit the final -e before adding -ly.

true	+ ly	=	truly
due	+ ly	=	duly

c

In words ending in -le you drop the final -le before adding -ly.

EXAMPLE

gentle   + ly   =   gently
▲   ▲
ends in -le   omit -le

Words like this are:

i) bristle   bristly
    crinkle   crinkly
    prickle   prickly
    tickle   tickly

ii) All the -able/-ible words when forming adverbs.

EXAMPLES

possible   + ly   =   possibly
enjoyable   + ly   =   enjoyably

(See page 63)

UNIT REVIEW EXERCISE

■ Add -ly to the following words using the above rules and exceptions.

dangerous	time	crinkle	terrible	busy
lucky	intense	tickle	easy	beautiful
needless	gentle	due	sincere	horrible
cosy	noisy	rare		

SENTENCE MAKERS

■ For each of the following words, make up a sentence of your own. Try to make your sentences interesting or funny.

sincerely	faithfully	gently	terribly	easily
lazily	mortally	carefully	truly	beautifully
luckily	usefully			

5 -MENT

a

RULE

When you add the suffix -ment to a root word the rule is the same whether the word ends in a vowel or a consonant. You simply add -ment to the word.

EXAMPLES

astonish	+ ment	=	astonishment
▲			
consonant			
puzzle	+ ment	=	puzzlement
▲			
vowel			

EXERCISE

■ Add -ment to the following words and write out the new words in your workbook.

achieve	advertise	agree	amuse	bewilder
catch	commence	commit	develop	embarrass
excite	govern	harass	invest	measure
move	nourish	pay	punish	puzzle
recruit	settle	state	treat	wonder

EXCEPTION

In the case of the word **argue** you drop the -e before adding -ment.

argue	+ ment	=	argument

EITHER/OR

The following words can *either* keep the -e *or* drop it before -ment.

judgement/judgment
acknowledgement/acknowledgment

b

There are a number of words you should know in which the suffix -ment is inseparable from the root word rather than added on.

Here is a list of the most useful words like this.

armament	casement	compartment	environment	figment
fitment	implement	instrument	increment	oddment
ointment	ornament	pavement	parliament	sacrament
sediment	segment	sentiment	supplement	tenement
testament	tournament			

EXERCISES

■ Write out each word from the above list *twice* in your workbook.

■ For each of the following words, make up a sentence of your own.

ointment   pavement   ornament   environment   compartment

SENTENCE MAKERS

■ Make up a sentence for each of the following words. Try to make your sentences interesting or funny.

advertisement	argument	environment	instrument
ointment	embarrassment	agreement	pavement
compartment	payment	arrangement	commitment

6 -ANCE/-ANT

a

There are a large number of *nouns* which end in -ance. You turn these words into *adjectives* by changing the -ance to -ant.

EXAMPLE

Noun	*Adjective*
arrogance	arrogant

EXERCISE

■ In your workbook write out the list of nouns and adjectives of the words below just like in the example given.

arrogance	assistance	attendance	brilliance	dominance
elegance	extravagance	exuberance	fragrance	ignorance
observance	radiance	relevance	repugnance	resistance
significance	vigilance			

EXAMPLE

Noun	*Adjective*
abundance	abundant

b Here is list of *nouns* ending in -ant which you should know.

accountant	applicant	assailant	assistant	attendant
defendant	elephant	emigrant	immigrant	inhabitant
lieutenant	merchant	militant	occupant	peasant
restaurant	sergeant	stimulant		

EXERCISES

■ Write out each word from the above list *twice* in your workbook.

■ For each of the following words, make up a sentence of your own. Try to make your sentences interesting or funny.

elephant attendant sergeant assistant defendant restaurant

SENTENCE MAKERS

■ For each of the following words, make up a sentence of your own. Try to make your sentences interesting or funny.

arrogant lieutenant brilliance fragrance occupant emigrant
merchant ignorant immigrant accountant assistance

7 -ENCE/-ENT

There are a large number of *nouns* which end in -ence. These words change the -ence to -ent when forming *adjectives*.

EXAMPLE

Noun	*Adjective*
absence	absent

EXERCISES

■ Here is a list of the most useful words like this. Write these words out in your workbook just like in the example given.

benevolence	coherence	confidence	dependence	difference
diligence	eminence	impudence	innocence	intelligence
negligence	obedience	patience	permanence	persistence
residence	reverence	silence	violence	

EXAMPLE

Noun   *Adjective*
absence   absent

■ Make up a sentence for each of the following words. Try to make your sentences interesting or funny.

innocent	dependent	difference	residence	violent
confident	permanent	silent	intelligent	presence
impudent	patient	obedience	prominent	

8 -ENSE

Here is a useful list of words ending in -ense.

dense	expense	immense	incense	license *(verb)*
nonsense	recompense	sense	suspense	tense

EXERCISES

■ Write out each word from the above list *twice* in your workbook.

■ Make up a sentence for each of the following words. Try to make your sentences interesting or funny.

sense   suspense   nonsense   dense   license   immense

9 -TION

A large number of words have the ending -tion. Here is a list of the most useful words like this.

accommodation	action	addition	ammunition
assassination	caution	celebration	communication
competition	composition	condition	conjunction
conversation	correction	creation	description
destruction	direction	education	emotion
examination	exception	exclamation	execution
exhibition	fiction	fraction	function
illustration	intention	invention	mention
nation	observation	operation	opposition
persecution	petition	population	position
qualification	question	reputation	satisfaction
sensation	situation	station	suggestion
temptation			

■ Write out each word from the above list *twice* in your workbook.

■ Pick *ten* words from the above list and make up a sentence of your own for each one.

10 -SION

Here is a useful list of words which end in -sion.

collision	comprehension	compulsion	conclusion	confusion
conversion	decision	dimension	division	erosion
exclusion	explosion	expulsion	extension	illusion
invasion	mansion	occasion	persuasion	provision
vision				

■ Write out each word from the above list *twice* in your workbook.

■ Pick *six* words from the above list and use each one in a sentence of your own.

NOTE

The word **suspicion** is spelt with a 'c'.

suspicion

11 -SSION

Here is a useful list of words ending in -ssion.

admission	commission	compassion	concession	concussion
depression	expression	impression	mission	obsession
omission	passion	permission	procession	succession
transmission				

■ Write out each word from the above list *twice* in your workbook.

■ Pick *five* words from the above list and then use each one in a sentence.

12   -FUL

a

RULE

In a large number of words -ful is simply added to a root word to make an adjective.

EXAMPLE

hope   + ful   =   hopeful
▲   ▲
noun   Note: single -l

EXCEPTION

Note that in the following words which end in double -l you drop one of the -l's before adding -ful.

skill   + ful   =   skilful
will   + ful   =   wilful

EXERCISE

■ Add -ful to the following words. Write this list out in your workbook.

art	cheer	colour	delight	dread	faith
fear	force	grace	harm	hope	joy
law	peace	purpose	right	shame	sorrow
success	thank	thought	truth	skill	use
waste	will	wrong	youth		

■ For each of the following words, make up a sentence of your own.

boastful	successful	graceful	wrongful	careful	skilful
cheerful	thankful	peaceful	colourful	rightful	delightful
useful	harmful	boastful			

b

RULE

When you add -ful to *words ending in* -y, you change the -y to an -i.

EXAMPLE

mercy   + ful   =   merciful
▲   ▲
ends in -y   change -y to -i

EXERCISE

■ Using the above rule add -ful to the following words.

beauty   duty   fancy   mercy   pity   plenty

13 **-LESS**

a

RULE

You can add -less to many words to make an adjective.

EXAMPLE

use   + less   =   useless

EXERCISE

■ Add -less to the following words to make adjectives.

bound	care	cease	change	cheer	colour
face	fault	fruit	hope	harm	law
name	need	noise	pain	price	sense
tact	taste	thought	use	weight	worth

b

RULE

When you add -less to a root word which ends in -y, you change the -y to an -i.

EXAMPLES

pity   + less   =   pitiless

mercy   + less   =   merciless

14 **-SOME**

Here is a useful list of words ending in -some.

awesome	cumbersome	fearsome	gruesome	handsome
tiresome	troublesome	winsome	quarrelsome	

■ Write out the above list of words *twice* in your workbook.
■ Use each of these words in a sentence.

15 -ARY/-ERY/-ORY

a WORDS ENDING IN -ARY

Here is a useful list of words which end in -ary.

adversary	anniversary	beneficiary	commentary	documentary
dictionary	elementary	exemplary	extraordinary	fragmentary
glossary	imaginary	infirmary	necessary	ordinary
primary	secondary	secretary	stationary *(standing still)*	
temporary				

EXERCISES
■ Write this list out *twice* in your workbook.
■ For each of the following words, make up a sentence of your own.

anniversary dictionary   infirmary   necessary stationary
primary   extraordinary temporary secretary secondary
imaginary

b WORDS ENDING IN -ERY

Here is a useful list of words which end in -ery.

adultery	battery	brewery	confectionery	crockery
discovery	distillery	embroidery	imagery	jewellery
machinery	periphery	recovery	stationery *(papers)*	

EXERCISES
■ Write out each word from the above list *three times* in your workbook.
■ For each of the following words, make up a sentence of your own.

confectionery jewellery recovery machinery discovery
embroidery

c

WORDS ENDING IN -ORY

Here is a useful list of words which end in -ory.

category   compulsory conservatory directory factory
inventory   lavatory   mandatory   obligatory observatory
promontory

74

EXERCISES

- Write out the above words *twice* in your workbook.
- For each of the following words, make up a sentence of your own. Try to make your sentences interesting or funny.

factory   directory   compulsory   obligatory

16   -AL/-EL/-IL

a

WORDS ENDING IN -AL

Here is a useful list of words which end in -al.

accidental   animal   cereal   crystal   decimal
educational eternal   fatal   formal   general
hospital   jackal   identical   incidental journal
local   logical   musical   mineral   national
petal   principal *(first/chief)*   personal *(of a person)*
rascal   rehearsal several   signal   total
typical   vertical

EXERCISES

- Write out each word from the above list *twice* in your workbook.
- For each of the following words, make up a sentence of your own.

fatal   typical   accidental hospital petals   several
total   local   cereal   musical

b

WORDS ENDING IN -IAL

Here is a useful list of words which end in -ial.

aerial   circumstantial confidential crucial   essential
facial   impartial   judicial   special

EXERCISES

■ Write out the above useful list of words ending in -ial *three times* in your workbook.

■ For each of the following words, make up a sentence of your own.

confidential   essential   special

c WORDS ENDING IN -UAL

Here is a useful list of words which end in -ual.

casual   eventual   habitual   individual   manual   usual

EXERCISE

■ Write out each word from the above list *three times* in your workbook.

d WORDS ENDING IN -EL

Here is a useful list of words which end in -el.

angel	barrel	camel	channel	chapel	chisel
colonel	duel	easel	enamel	fuel	hazel
hostel	hotel	jewel	label	lapel	level
mackerel	model	navel	novel	panel	parcel
personnel *(staff)*		quarrel	rebel	spaniel	tinsel
towel	travel	vessel			

EXERCISES

■ Write out each word from the above list *twice* in your workbook.

■ For each of the following words, make up a sentence of your own.

travel	barrels	jewels	camels	model	quarrel
parcel	vessels	fuel	label	level	spaniel

e WORDS ENDING IN -IL

Here is a useful list of words which end in -il.

pupil   stencil   tendril   tonsils   utensil   vigil

EXERCISE
- Write out each word from the above list *twice* in your workbook.

17 -OR/-AR/-ER

a WORDS ENDING IN -OR

Here is a useful list of words ending in -or.

actor	author	calculator	competitor	conductor
conjuror	conspirator	director	doctor	exterior
factor	indicator	inferior	inspector	instructor
major	manor	minor	mirror	motor
narrator	operator	professor	projector	radiator
refrigerator	sailor	survivor	tenor	traitor
tutor	victor			

EXERCISES
- Write out each word from the above list *twice* in your workbook.
- For each of the following words, make up a sentence of your own.

exterior traitor   sailor   victors   calculator doctor
actor   inspectors conjuror competitor director   mirror

b WORDS ENDING IN -AR

Here is a useful list of words ending in -ar.

altar *(in church)*		beggar	burglar	calendar	caterpillar
cellar	circular	collar	familiar	grammar	guitar
particular	peculiar	pillar	popular	regular	scholar
similar	singular	solar	sonar	vinegar	

EXERCISES
- Write out the above list of words ending in -ar twice in your workbook.
- For each of the following words, make up a sentence of your own.

beggars   regular   similar   guitar   calendar   peculiar
circular   popular

c

WORDS ENDING IN -ER

Here is a useful list of words ending in -er which are the names of *people* or their *occupations*.

announcer	baker	butcher	brother	carer	carpenter
carrier	cashier	coroner	employer	farmer	father
foreigner	gardener	mariner	mother	passenger	sister
soldier	traveller				

EXERCISES

■ Write out each word from the above list *twice* in your workbook.

■ For each of the following words, make up a sentence of your own.

sister	foreigner	butcher	soldier	cashier	brother
passengers	travellers	father	mother		

d

Here is a useful list of other words which end in -er.

alter *(change)*	answer	bitter	butter	character
conquer	cylinder	hammer	ladder	leather
manner	order	pepper	register	remember
saucer	slaughter	spider	surrender	terrier
tower	weather			

EXERCISES

■ Write out each word from the above list *twice* in your workbook.

■ For each of the following words, make up a sentence of your own.

farmer	answer	pepper	weather	saucer	terrier
spiders	surrender				

18 **-IC**

a

Here is a useful list of words ending in -ic.

basic	characteristic	classic	comic	cosmetic
critic	domestic	dynamic	economic	elastic
electric	emphatic	fanatic	fantastic	frantic
garlic	gigantic	hectic	heroic	magic
mimic	panic	pathetic	Olympic	organic
republic	romantic	sarcastic	scenic	scientific
specific	tactic	tonic	tragic	tunic

b

RULE

To form an adverb from a word ending in **-ic** you add **-ally**.

EXAMPLE

basic   + ally   =   basically

NOTE

When **panic** is a verb you add **-k** before an ending or suffix beginning with a vowel.

panic   panicked   panicking

EXERCISES

■ Write out each word from the above list in your workbook.

■ Add **-ally** to the following words in your workbook.

pathetic   comic   tragic   basic   critic   emphatic
characteristic classic   sarcastic

■ For each of the following words, make up a sentence of your own.

magically   basic   cosmetics   tunic   frantically sarcastic
scenic   fanatic electric   heroic   tactically   organic
panicked

19 **-IST/-ISM**

Here is a useful list of words which end in **-ist** or **-ism**.

botanist   cellist   chemist   chiropodist environmentalist
evangelist extremism   florist   machinist   naturalist
pacifist   perfectionist pessimism protagonist oculist
optimist   royalist   sadism   scientist   stylist
tourism   ventriloquist

EXERCISES

■ Write out each word from the above list in your workbook.

■ For each of the following words, make up a sentence of your own.

chemist   extremist   florist   tourism   ventriloquist
pessimist   scientist   perfectionist optimism

20 -LOGY

Here is a useful list of words ending in -logy.

anthology	anthropology	apology	biology	chronology
cosmology	ecology	etymology	geology	meteorology
mythology	physiology	psychology	sociology	technology
theology	zoology			

EXERCISES

■ Write out the following useful list of words ending in -logy in your workbook.

■ For each of the following words, make up a sentence of your own.

apology technology ecology geology cosmology biology

NOTE

Remember that when you use these words in the plural you change the -y to -ie before adding -s.

For example,

apologies   technologies   (see page 57)

21 -GRAPHY

Here is a useful list of words ending in -graphy.

| autobiography | biography | choreography | geography |
| oceanography | orthography | photography | radiography |

EXERCISES

■ Write out the above list of words ending in -graphy in your workbook.

PART 7

Double Consonants

This unit deals with lists of words containing double consonants.
The lists are based on the most commonly used words as well as
those words which give difficulties.

1

WORDS CONTAINING -BB-

Here is a useful list of words containing -bb-.

abbey	abbot	babble	bobbin	bubble	cabbage
chubby	dabble	dribble	ebb	flabby	gibbon
gobble	hobble	hobby	jabber	nibble	pebble
rabbi	rabbit	rabble	ribbon	robber	rubber
rubbish	rubble	shabby	squabble	stubble	stubborn

EXERCISES

■ Write out each word from the above list *twice* in your
workbook.

■ For each of the following words, make up a sentence of your
own. Try to make your sentences interesting or funny.

babbling	nibbled	rubbish	shabby	cabbage	pebble
flabby	robbers	stubborn	rabbit	hobbies	squabbling

2

WORDS CONTAINING -CC-

Here is a useful list of words containing -cc-.

accelerate	accept	accessory	accident
acclaim	accommodation	accomplish	accordingly
accumulation	accurate	broccoli	eccentric
hiccup	impeccable	moccasin	piccolo
occasion	occupy	occur	succeed
success	succulent	tobacco	vaccinate

EXERCISES

■ Write out each word from the above list *twice* in your workbook.

■ For each of the following words, make up a sentence of your own. Try to make your sentences interesting or funny.

acceleration	eccentric	hiccups	moccasins	accepted
occasionally	accidentally	occupied	successful	
accommodated	tobacco	accurately		

3 WORDS CONTAINING -DD-

Here is a useful list of words containing **-dd-**.

add	adder	address	befuddle	bladder	cuddle
fiddle	giddy	huddle	ladder	middle	muddle
paddle	pudding	puddle	oddity	redden	riddle
rudder	shudder	sudden	swaddle	twiddle	udder
waddle	wedding				

EXERCISES

■ Write out each word from the above list *twice* in your workbook.

■ For each of the following words, make up a sentence of your own. Try to make your sentences interesting or funny.

adding	muddled	shuddered	riddles	addressed	pudding
wedding	fiddled	cuddled	ladders	middle	suddenly

4 WORDS WITH -FF-

a WORDS ENDING IN -FF

Here is a useful list of words ending in **-ff**.

bluff	cliff	dandruff	gruff	midriff	sheriff
sniff	staff	stiff	stuff	tiff	whiff

EXERCISES

■ Write out each word from the above list *twice* in your workbook.

■ For each of the following words, make up a sentence of your own. Try to make your sentences interesting or funny.

bluffed	sniffed	stuffing	staff	cliffs	stiff
sheriff	whiff	gruffly			

b WORDS CONTAINING -FF-

Here is a useful list of words containing -ff-.

affair	affection	affix	afflict	afford	baffling
buffalo	buffer	buffet	coffee	coffin	daffodil
difficult	efface	effort	giraffe	muffler	offend
offer	office	paraffin	raffle	ruffian	ruffle
scaffold	scruffy	scuffle	suffer	suffice	suffix
suffocate	toffee	traffic	waffle		

EXERCISES

■ Write out each word from the above list *twice* in your workbook.

■ For each of the following words, make up a sentence of your own. Try to make your sentences interesting or funny.

affectionately	giraffe	scruffy	suffered	afford
attended	coffee	daffodils	traffic	office
difficulty	effortless			

5 WORDS CONTAINING -GG-

Here is a useful list of words containing -gg-.

aggravate	aggression	baggage	beggar	dagger
exaggerate	giggle	groggy	haggard	haggis
juggler	luggage	maggot	nugget	reggae
rugged	smuggle	stagger	struggle	suggest
swagger	toboggan	trigger	wriggle	

EXERCISES

■ Write out each word from the above list *twice* in your workbook.

■ For each of the following words, make up a sentence of your own. Try to make your sentences interesting or funny.

aggressor	giggling	trigger	luggage	beggars
haggis	juggler	suggest	dagger	exaggerate
smuggler	wriggled			

6 WORDS WITH -LL-

a WORDS ENDING IN -LL

Here is a useful list of words which end in -ll.

ball	bell	bill	bull	call	cell
doll	dull	dwell	fell	fill	full
mill	pill	pull	quell	roll	shall
smell	spell	still	stroll	tell	trill
will					

EXERCISES

■ Write out each word from the above list *twice* in your workbook.

■ For each of the following words, make up a sentence of your own. Try to make your sentences interesting or funny.

ball	filling	smells	called	rolling	shall
strolled	dullest	tell	full	willing	bills

b WORDS CONTAINING -LL-

Here is a useful list of words containing -ll-.

alley	allow	ally	ballad	ballet	balloon
ballot	billiards	brilliant	bullet	cello	challenge
chilly	collect	college	dolly	fellow	follow
gallon	gazelle	gorilla	Halloween	hollow	holly
illustration	intellect	jelly	jolly	killer	lollipop
lullaby	mellow	miller	parallel	penicillin	pellet
pulley	rally	rebellion	shallow	stallion	sullen
thriller	trolley	umbrella	valley	vanilla	village
villain	volley	wallet	willow	yellow	

EXERCISES

■ Write out the above useful list of words in your workbook.

■ For each of the following words, make up a sentence of your own. Try to make your sentences interesting or funny.

followed	galleon	rebellion	hollows	parallel	challenged
stallion	chilly	thriller	yellow	sullenly	lollipop

7 WORDS CONTAINING -MM-

Here is a useful list of words containing -mm-.

accommodation	ammonia	ammunition	comma
command	commend	comment	commitment
common	commotion	flammable	gammon
glimmer	grammar	hammer	immediate
immense	immune	mammal	recommend
simmer	summary	summer	summit
summon			

EXERCISES

- Write out each word from the above list *twice* in your workbook.
- For each of the following words, make up a sentence of your own. Try to make your sentences interesting or funny.

ammunition	commanded	glimmered	hammering
comments	immediately	immense	simmering
committed	accommodation	summer	commotion

8 WORDS CONTAINING -NN-

Here is a useful list of words containing -nn-.

anniversary	announce	annoy	annual
banner	bunny	cannibal	cannon
cannot	channel	connection	flannel
funnel	funny	inner	kennel
innocent	Madonna	mannequin	manner
mayonnaise	minnow	nanny	personnel *(staff)*
questionnaire	runner	spanner	tennis
tunnel	uncanny	winnow	

EXERCISES

- Write out each word from the above list *twice* in your workbook.
- For each of the following words, make up a sentence of your own. Try to make your sentences interesting or funny.

funniest	anniversary	innocent	annoys
manners	personnel *(staff)*	questionnaire	cannot
tunnelled	mayonnaise	tennis	connected

9 WORDS CONTAINING -PP-

Here is a useful list of words containing -pp-.

appalling	apparatus	apparent	appeal
appear	appetite	apple	apply
appoint	appreciate	approach	approve
approximately	cripple	happen	happy
hippopotamus	opponent	opportunity	oppose
opposite	oppress	pepper	puppet
ripple	stoppage	supper	supple
supply	support	suppose	suppress
topple	upper		

85

EXERCISES

■ Write out each word from the above list *twice* in your workbook.

■ For each of the following words, make up a sentence of your own. Try to make your sentences interesting or funny.

appealed	appearance	happily	appetite	happened
puppets	supper	supporters	apples	opposed
ripples	appreciate			

10 WORDS CONTAINING -RR-

Here is a useful list of words containing -rr-.

arrange	arrears	arrest	arrive
arrow	barrel	barren	barrier
barrow	carriage	carrot	carry
correct	correspond	corrupt	currant *(fruit)*
current *(electricity)*	curriculum	curry	earring
embarrass	error	ferry	furrow
garrison	horrid	horrified	horror
marriage	Mediterranean	merry	mirror
narrow	occurrence	purr	quarry
resurrection	squirrel	surrender	surround
terrace	terrible	terrier	terror
tomorrow	warren	warrior	worry

EXERCISES

■ Write out each word from the above list *twice* in your workbook.

■ For each of the following words, make up a sentence of your own. Try to make your sentences interesting or funny.

arranged	earrings	currants	married	arrested	narrowly
carrying	embarrassed	terrified	barrels	curry	worried

11 WORDS WITH -SS-

86 **a** WORDS ENDING IN -SS

Here is a useful list of words which end in -ss.

abbess	abscess	assess	baroness	bless	bliss
bypass	caress	chess	class	compass	confess
countess	digress	dismiss	duchess	embarrass	excess
express	fortress	goddess	harass	harness	hiss
impress	kiss	morass	progress	stress	success
surpass	toss	trespass	unless		

EXERCISES

■ Write out each word from the above list *twice* in your workbook.

■ For each of the following words, make up a sentence of your own. Try to make your sentences interesting or funny.

blessing	kissing	fortress	impressed	blissfully
stressed	expression	successfully	confessed	dismissed
unless	embarrassing			

b WORDS CONTAINING -SS-.

Here is a useful list of words containing -ss-.

assassin	assault	assemble	assign	assist
blossom	casserole	cassette	crevasse	croissant
delicatessen	dissect	dissuade	embassy	finesse
fissure	fossil	glossary	gossamer	hassle
incessant	lasso	lesson	massacre	massage
massive	message	missile	mission	mousse
necessity	obsessed	possess	rissole	russet
session				

EXERCISES

■ Write out the above useful list of words *twice* in your workbook.

■ For each of the following words, make up a sentence of your own. Try to make your sentences interesting or funny.

assassinated	lessons	missiles	massive	assistant	messages
casserole	possessed	necessary	cassette	fossils	assaulted

WORDS CONTAINING -TT-

12

Here is a useful list of words containing -tt-.

attack	attain	attempt	attention	attitude	attract
battle	better	bottle	bottom	butter	button
cigarette	confetti	cottage	cotton	ditto	glitter
glutton	jetty	kitten	latter	launderette	litter
matter	mutton	omelette	otter	platter	shutter
titter	totter	twitter	witter		

87

EXERCISES

■ Write out each word from the above list *twice* in your workbook.

■ For each of the following words, make up a sentence of your own. Try to make your sentences interesting or funny.

attacked	better	glittering	attention	utterly	kittens
buttered	cigarettes	bottles	attractive	battles	matter

WORDS CONTAINING -ZZ-

13

blizzard	buzz	dazzle	dizzy	drizzle	embezzle
fizzy	frizzle	fuzzy	guzzle	jazz	muzzle
nozzle	nuzzle	pizza	puzzle	quizzical	sizzle

EXERCISES

■ Write out the following list of words *twice* in your workbook.

■ For each of the following words, make up a sentence of your own. Try to make your sentences interesting or funny.

blizzard	muzzled	dizzy	sizzling	buzzing	pizza
jazz	puzzled	fizzy			

PART 8

Consonant Clusters

1 WORDS CONTAINING -SC-

The -sc- cluster in a word is pronounced in three different ways:

- a) like 'ss' as in 'science';
- b) like 'sk' as in 'scarce';
- c) like 'sh' as in 'crescendo'.

We will group the -sc- words according to the way the -sc- is pronounced.

a Here is a useful list of words in which -sc- is pronounced like 'ss'.

abscess	ascend	ascension	crescent	descend
discern	disciple	discipline	fascinate	miscellaneous
reminiscence	scene	scent	sceptic	science
scimitar	scissors			

EXERCISES

■ Write out each word from the above list *twice* in your workbook.

■ For each of the following words, make up a sentence of your own. Try to make your sentences interesting or funny.

ascending   scientific   abscess   scenic   crescent   discipline descended   fascination

b Here is a useful list of words in which -sc- is pronounced like 'sk'.

biscuit	discus *(sport)*	discuss *(talk)*	escape	manuscript
mascara	mascot	scab	scaffold	scald
scale	scalp	scan	scandal	scar
scare	scarlet	scatter	scoff	scold
scone	scorch	score	scorn	scoundrel
scowl	scrap	scrape	scratch	scrawl
screech	screen	screw	script	scripture
scrounge	scrub	scruffy	scuff	sculptor
scum	scurry			

EXERCISE

■ Write out each word from the above list *twice* in your workbook.

c Here is a useful list of words in which -sc- is pronounced like 'sh'.

conscience   conscientious   conscientiously   crescendo

EXERCISES

■ Write out each word from the above list *twice* in your workbook.

■ For each of the above words, make up a sentence. Try to make your sentences interesting or funny.

2 WORDS CONTAINING -GH-

The -gh- cluster in a word is pronounced in four different ways:
    a) pronounced 'ff'
    b) pronounced hard 'g'
    c) silent 'gh'
    d) pronounced as in the word **burgh** which rhymes with **mirror**.

We will group the -gh- words according to the way the -gh- is pronounced.

a Here is a useful list of words in which -gh- is pronounced 'ff'.

cough   enough   laugh   rough   tough   trough

b Here is a useful list of words in which -gh- is pronounced with a hard 'g'.

aghast   dinghy   ghastly   ghetto   ghost   ghoul

c Here is a useful list of words in which -gh- is silent.

although borough bough   dough   high   plough
sigh   sleigh   thigh   thorough though through
weigh

d The word **burgh** contains -gh- and rhymes with **mirror**.

EXERCISES

■ Write out each of the lists of words in a), b), c) and d) above *twice* in your workbook.

■ For each of the following words, make up a sentence. Try to make your sentences interesting or funny.

although	coughing	ghosts	ploughman	roughly
laughing	thoroughly	toughness	weighed	through

3 WORDS CONTAINING -GHT-

a Here is a useful list of words containing -ight-.

almighty	blight	bright	eight	fight	flight
freight	height	knight	light	lightning	might
mighty	plight	right	sight	slight	straight
tight	tonight	twilight	upright	uptight	weight

b Here is a list of words containing -aught-.

caught	daughter	distraught	draught	onslaught	haughty
naughty	slaughter	taught			

c Here is a useful list of words ending in -ought.

bought	brought	drought	fought	nought	ought
sought	thought				

EXERCISES

■ Write out each list of words in a), b) and c) above *twice* in your workbook.

■ For each of the following words, make up a sentence. Try to make your sentences interesting or funny.

lightning	might	ought	brightly	straightened	right
sight	caught	eighteen	tonight	weight	

4 WORDS WITH -GU-

a WORDS BEGINNING WITH GU-

Here is a useful list of words beginning with **gu-**.

guarantee	guard	guardian	guerilla	guess	guidance
guild	guile	guillotine	guilt	guinea-pig	guise
guitar					

EXERCISES

■ Write out each word from the above list *twice* in your workbook.

■ For each of the following words, make up a sentence. Try to make your sentences interesting or funny.

guaranteed guerilla guard dog guessing guilty guitars

b WORDS CONTAINING -GU-

Here is a useful list of words containing **-gu-**.

baguette	beguile	distinguish	extinguish	language
languid	languish	languor		

EXERCISES

■ Write out each word from the above list *twice* in your workbook.

■ For each of the following words, make up a sentence. Try to make your sentences interesting or funny.

distinguishing languages extinguished baguettes

c WORDS ENDING IN -GUE

Here is a useful list of words ending in **-gue**.

catalogue	colleague	dialogue	fatigue	harangue
intrigue	league	monologue	morgue	plague
prologue	rogue	synagogue	tongue	travelogue

EXERCISES

■ Write out each word from the above list *twice* in your workbook.

■ For each of the following words, make up a sentence. Try to make your sentences interesting or funny.

catalogue tongue fatigued rogues colleagues dialogue

5 WORDS BEGINNING WITH WH-

Here is a useful list of words beginning with wh-.

whack	whale	wheat	wheedle	wheel
when	wherever	where	whet	which
whiff	while	whim	whimper	whine
whip	whisk	whisker	whisky	whisper
whist	white	whiz	who	whoever
whole	wholesome	whom	whose	why

EXERCISES

■ Write out each word from the above list *twice* in your workbook.

■ For each of the following words, make up a sentence. Try to make your sentences interesting or funny.

where	whimpering	wheels	who	when	whales
whining	whose	why	whispering	which	whom

6 WORDS WITH -QU-

a WORDS BEGINNING WITH QU-

Here is a useful list of words beginning with qu-.

quack	quaint	qualification	qualify	quality
quantity	quarrel	quarter	queen	queer
quench	question	questionnaire	queue	quick
quiet	quit	quite	quiz	quotation

EXERCISES

■ Write out each word from the above list *twice* in your workbook.

■ For each of the following words, make up a sentence. Try to make your sentences interesting or funny.

qualifications	queer	quickly	quarrelled	quietly
questions	quarter	queen	quiz	

b

WORDS CONTAINING -QU-

Here is a useful list of words containing -qu-.

bequeath	bequest	delinquent	equal	eloquent
equator	frequent	liquid	mosquito	relinquish
request	requiem	sequel	sequin	squabble
square	squash	squawk	squeeze	squid
squint	tranquil	vanquish	ventriloquist	

9:

EXERCISES

■ Write out each word from the above list *twice* in your workbook.

■ For each of the following words, make up a sentence. Try to make your sentences interesting or funny.

equalled	frequently	squashed	squinting	squeeze
square	eloquent	squabble	ventriloquist	

c

WORDS ENDING IN -QUE

Here is a useful list of words ending in -que.

antique	boutique	cheque	clique	grotesque
mosque	mystique	oblique	opaque	physique
picturesque	pique	statuesque	technique	unique

EXERCISES

■ Write out the above list of words *twice* in your workbook.

■ For each of the following words, make up a sentence. Try to make your sentences interesting or funny.

unique   cheque-book   mosque   boutique   picturesque

7   WORDS WITH -PH-

a   WORDS BEGINNING WITH PH-

Here is a useful list of words beginning with ph-.

phantom	pharmacy	pheasant	phenomenal	philosophy
phoenix	phone	phosphorous	photograph	physical
physician	physics			

EXERCISE

■ Write out each word from the above list *twice* in your workbook.

Consonant Clusters

94

b WORDS CONTAINING -PH-

Here is a useful list of words containing -ph-.

alphabet	amphibian	atmosphere	biography	catastrophe
decipher	elephant	emphasis	geography	hemisphere
hyphen	metaphor	microphone	morphine	nephew
orphan	pamphlet	prophet	siphon	sphere
sulphate	sulphur	symphony	telephone	typhoid
typhoon				

EXERCISES

- Write out each word from the above list *twice* in your workbook.

- For each of the following words, make up a sentence. Try to make your sentences interesting or funny.

  alphabet elephant telephone geography catastrophe
  nephew orphans emphatic metaphor

c WORDS ENDING IN -PH

Here is a useful list of words ending in -ph.

cenotaph epitaph paragraph photograph telegraph triumph

EXERCISE

- Write out each word from the above list *twice* in your workbook.

8 WORDS ENDING IN -DGE

Here is a useful list of words ending in -dge.

badge	bridge	cartridge	dodge	dredge	edge
fridge	fudge	grudge	hedge	judge	knowledge
ledge	lodge	nudge	partridge	pledge	porridge
ridge	sledge	sludge	smudge	stodge	trudge

EXERCISES

- Write out each word from the above list *twice* in your workbook.

- For each of the following words, make up a sentence. Try to make your sentences interesting or funny.

  bridge edges pledged hedges ridge smudging
  cartridge grudge nudged

9 WORDS ENDING IN -LE

a WORDS ENDING IN -GLE

Here is a useful list of words ending in -gle.

angle	bangle	bungle	dangle	eagle	gargle
jingle	jungle	mangle	mingle	ogle	rectangle
shingle	single	smuggle	spangle	struggle	tangle
triangle	wangle	wriggle			

EXERCISES

■ Write out each word from the above list *twice* in your workbook.

■ For each of the following words, make up a sentence. Try to make your sentences interesting or funny.

struggled   jungle   angles   eagle   triangle   wriggling
mingled   smuggler

b WORDS ENDING IN -PLE

Here is a useful list of words ending in -ple.

couple	maple	multiple	participle	people	pimple
principle	purple	sample	scruple	staple	steeple
temple					

EXERCISES

■ Write out each word from the above list *twice* in your workbook.

■ For each of the following words, make up a sentence. Try to make your sentences interesting or funny.

couple   people   purple   samples   temples   steeple
principles   pimple

c WORDS ENDING IN -PPLE

Here is a useful list of words ending in -pple.

  apple nipple ripple stipple supple tipple

EXERCISES

- Write out each word from the above list *twice* in your workbook.
- For each of the following words, make up a sentence. Try to make your sentences interesting or funny.

 apples   supple   ripples

d WORDS ENDING IN -CLE

Here is a useful list of words ending in -cle.

  bicycle cycle icicle manacle muscle obstacle
  receptacle tentacle treacle

EXERCISES

- Write out each word from the above list *twice* in your workbook.
- For each of the following words, make up a sentence. Try to make your sentences interesting or funny.

 treacle   icicle   muscle   bicycle

e WORDS ENDING IN -KLE

Here is a useful list of words ending in -kle.

  sparkle sprinkle twinkle winkle wrinkle

EXERCISES

- Write out each word from the above list *twice* in your workbook.
- For each of the following words, make up a sentence. Try to make your sentences interesting or funny.

 wrinkles   sparkle   twinkle   sprinkled

f

WORDS ENDING IN -CKLE

Here is a useful list of words ending in **-ckle**.

pickle   prickle   shackle   sickle   speckle   suckle

tackle   tickle   trickle

EXERCISES

■ Write out each word from the above list *twice* in your workbook.

■ For each of the following words, make up a sentence. Try to make your sentences interesting or funny.

pickles   tackled   trickled   speckled   suckled   tickled

g

WORDS ENDING IN -DLE

Here is a useful list of words ending in **-dle**.

bundle   candle   cradle   curdle   doodle   girdle

handle   hurdle   idle   ladle   needle   noodle

poodle   spindle   swindle

EXERCISES

■ Write out each word from the above list *twice* in your workbook.

■ For each of the following words, make up a sentence. Try to make your sentences interesting or funny.

candle   handled   ladle   noodles   swindler   idle

h

WORDS ENDING IN -DDLE

Here is a useful list of words ending in **-ddle**.

cuddle   fiddle   fuddle   huddle   meddle   middle

paddle   peddle   riddle   saddle   straddle   twiddle

waddle

EXERCISES

■ Write out each word from the above list *twice* in your workbook.

■ For each of the following words, make up a sentence. Try to make your sentences interesting or funny.

fiddle   meddle   riddles   saddle   cuddle

straddled   middle   paddle

i

WORDS ENDING IN -TLE

Here is a useful list of words ending in -tle.

beetle	bristle	castle	dismantle	gentle	jostle
rustle	startle	subtle	thistle	title	whistle
wrestle					

98

EXERCISE

■ Write out each word from the above list *twice* in your workbook.

■ For each of the above words, make up a sentence. Try to make your sentences interesting or funny.

j

WORDS ENDING IN -TTLE

Here is a useful list of words ending in -ttle.

battle	bottle	fettle	kettle	rattle	scuttle
settle	shuttle	skittle	throttle	wattle	

EXERCISE

■ Write out each word from the above list *twice* in your workbook.

■ For each of the following words, make up a sentence. Try to make your sentences interesting or funny.

battled	bottles	rattle	settled	throttled	kettle

k

WORDS ENDING IN -BLE

Here is a useful list of words ending in -ble.

able	cable	delectable	gable	gamble	garble
humble	jumble	marble	mumble	nimble	noble
possible	ramble	rumble	scramble	stable	stumble
syllable	thimble	tremble	trouble	tumble	visible
warble					

See pages 60 to 63 for other -able/-ible words.

EXERCISES

■ Write out each word from the above list *twice* in your workbook.

■ For each of the following words, make up a sentence. Try to make your sentences interesting or funny.

able	trembling	stumbled	humble	nobles	mumbling
possible	delectable	visible		

1 WORDS ENDING IN -BBLE

Here is a useful list of words ending in -bble.

babble	bubble	gabble	gobble	hobble	nibble
pebble	rabble	rubble	scribble	squabble	wobble

EXERCISES

■ Write out each word from the above list *twice* in your workbook.

■ For each of the following words, make up a sentence. Try to make your sentences interesting or funny.

nibbled	pebbles	scribbled	rubble	wobbled

10 WORDS CONTAINING -TCH-

Here is a useful list of words containing -tch-.

batch	butcher	catch	clutch	ditch	etch
hatch	hatchet	hitch	hutch	itch	ketch
ketchup	kitchen	latch	match	notch	patch
pitch	satchel	scratch	snatch	sketch	stitch
stretch	switch	thatch	twitch	watch	witch
wretch					

EXERCISES

■ Write out each word from the above list *twice* in your workbook.

■ For each of the following words, make up a sentence. Try to make your sentences interesting or funny.

kitchen	catch	itching	witches	matching
clutched	watch	scratch	pitched	

PART 9

Silent Consonants

There are a large number of words which have unpronounced or silent consonants. Though these letters are not sounded separately they do sometimes affect the pronunciation of the rest of the word.

1 SILENT 'P'

Word list

pneumatic	pneumonia	psalm	psychiatrist
psychic	psychology	receipt	

EXERCISES

■ Write out each word from the above list *twice* in your workbook.

■ For each of the following words, make up a sentence. Try to make your sentences interesting or funny.

receipt   pneumonia   psalms

2 SILENT 'B'

Word list

bomb	climb	comb	crumb	debt	doubt
dumb	jamb	lamb	limb	numb	plumb
plumber	subtle	succumb	thumb	tomb	womb

EXERCISES

■ Write out each word from the above list *twice* in your workbook.

■ For each of the following words, make up a sentence. Try to make your sentences interesting or funny.

bomber	debts	subtle	lambs	climbed	doubtful
crumbs	plumber	tomb			

3 SILENT 'N'

Word list

autumn	column	condemn	damn	hymn	solemn

EXERCISES

■ Write out each word from the above list *twice* in your workbook.

■ For each of the following words, make up a sentence. Try to make your sentences interesting or funny.

autumn	solemn	hymns	condemned	columns

4 SILENT 'G'

Word list

align	alignment	campaign	champagne	deign
design	feign	foreign	gnarled	gnash
gnat	gnaw	gnome	gnu	malign
reign	resign	sign	sovereign	

EXERCISES

■ Write out each word from the above list *twice* in your workbook.

■ For each of the following words, make up a sentence. Try to make your sentences interesting or funny.

campaign	signed	gnat	gnawing	foreign
resigned	design	champagne		

5 | SILENT 'L'

Word list

balm	calm	embalm	palm	psalm	qualm
salmon	walk	yolk			

EXERCISES

■ Write out each word from the above list *twice* in your workbook.

■ For each of the following words, make up a sentence. Try to make your sentences interesting or funny.

calmly	qualms	yolk	salmon	walking	palm

6 | SILENT 'W'

Word list

wrangle	wrap	wreath	wreck	wren	wrestle
wretch	wriggle	wring	wrinkle	wrist	write
wrong					

EXERCISES

■ Write out each word from the above list *twice* in your workbook.

■ For each of the following words, make up a sentence. Try to make your sentences interesting or funny.

wrapper	wrist	watch	writing	wrinkles	wriggled
wretch	wrecks	wrestler			

PART 10

Unusual Words

Here is a useful list of unusual words, many of them foreign.

abyss	aerobics	aerosol	algebra	baguette
biscuit	bizarre	blancmange	boutique	calorie
camouflage	chauffeur	chauffeuse	chauvinist	connoisseur
cygnet	dahlia	debris	decaffeinated	decathlon
deuce	dungeon	Fahrenheit	fiasco	goulash
gourmet	gymkhana	gypsy	gyroscope	haiku
hydrogen	hygiene	kayak	labyrinth	lacquer
liaison	lieutenant	lingerie	lozenge	lynch
lynx	martyr	medieval	mediocre	mistletoe
nymph	pygmy	pyjamas	python	quartz
restaurant	oyster	sandwich	scythe	sergeant
shampoo	silhouette	souvenir	spaghetti	stalactite
stalagmite	suede	surgeon	surveillance	sycamore
synagogue	sword	tandoori	theatre	thyme
toupee	tuition	turquoise	vacuum	vehicle
venue	versatile	violin	virtue	waltz
witch	yacht	zebra	zinc	zither

EXERCISE

■ Pick out *fifteen* words from the above list and make up a sentence for each. Write these sentences in your workbook.

biscuit

restaurant

witch

silhouette

sword

yacht

gypsy

pyjamas

sandwich

spaghetti

theatre

vehicle

Notes

Notes